Mohammed Ameer Ali

The Moslem Festivities

Mohammed Ameer Ali

The Moslem Festivities

ISBN/EAN: 9783741103391

Manufactured in Europe, USA, Canada, Australia, Japa

Cover: Foto ©Lupo / pixelio.de

Manufactured and distributed by brebook publishing software
(www.brebook.com)

Mohammed Ameer Ali

The Moslem Festivities

THE

MOSLEM FESTIVITIES

BY

MOULVIE ABUL ANWAR SYED

MOHAMMED AMEER ALI

OF

(Bariawl, Durbhungah, Behar.)

Calcutta

PRINTED AND PUBLISHED FOR THE AUTHOR AND PROPRIETOR BY

MESSRS. H. C. GANGOOLY & CO.,

12, MANGOE LANE

1892.

No. 2802 P.

OFFICE MEMORANDUM.

POLITICAL DEPARTMENT.

Calcutta, the 12th August 1891.

With reference to his letter dated the 13th ultimo, submitting for transmission to the Government of India, in the Home Department, an application for permission to publish a portrait of Her Majesty the Queen-Empress in his book entitled "The Moslem Festivities" which is said to be in press, Moulvie Syed Mohamed Ameer Ali is informed that he should renew his application with a copy of his work when it is ready.

(Sd.) H. LUSON,
Under Secretary to the
Government of Bengal.

To
ABUL ANWAR MOULVIE SYED
MOHAMMED AMEER ALI,
19, *Ripon Lane, Calcutta.*
or Village Barumi,
via Durbhungah.

In a position hereafter to publish a second edition of the book. He shall, however, in the meantime be happy to receive at any time portraits from gentlemen intending to favour him with them with the object of publication.

In conclusion, the author begs to thankfully acknowledge the kindly gifts of portraits from the Hon'ble Sir Steuart Colvin Bayley, K. C. S. I., and * Their Highnesses the worthy Nawabs Bahadurs Sir Abdul Gani, K. C. I. S., and the Hon'ble Nawab Ahsanullah Bahadoor, C. I. E., of Dacca, who are entitled to his grateful thanks for the same.

19, RIPON LANE,
CALCUTTA,
31st January 1892.
} THE AUTHOR.

---

* See the Postscript page 66 and its foot-notes containing the Nawab's two letters *anent* their donations and gifts of portraits for this pamphlet.

A REQUEST.

———

ALL our writings in these pages being *defacto bona fide* and based in every way upon the very texts and true fundamental principles of Islam, the authour does not feel himself called upon to add here anything as to accuracy of all that the book contains. He shall, however, be at all times ready and happy to receive any suggestions, and attend to all additions corrections and alterations, &c., which the reading public may hereafter like to favour him with for including in and omitting from this pamphlet ; and which he shall certainly make use of in the second edition.

THE AUTHOR.

PREFACE.

It is for the first time that the author ventures to appear before the Public with this little pamphlet, dealing with Mohammedan usages ; most of which are, he believes, hitherto unknown to the foreign reading public. The author has taken great pains in collecting materials—the subject matter of this little work—from Arabic and other Oriental books. These are the only references he has made for the purposes of this pamphlet ; and he earnestly hopes that his labour and a good portion of his valuable time devoted to this object, will be welcomed by the generous public at large. If this *brochure* meets with general encouragement, support, and sympathy, it may deserve, the author hopes to be able to enlarge it in a subsequent edition.

The total absence of any English work touching the subjects herein dealt with, has stood much in the author's way of success in making his writing more explicit than what it is now. He, therefore, feels constrained to admit the shortcomings this book contains, and its obvious incompleteness in various respects.

The author trusts that this book will in some measure supply the want which has hitherto existed for the absence of any work in the English language.

· The Author.

CONTENTS.

ii

CONTENTS.—*Continued.*

THE AKIKA.[*]

Akika, a pure Arabic word, literally means to indicate the naming of a person, or the cropping of one's hair. Religiously, it signifies and specifies a well-known weighty usage or rite observed in the families of all Mussulmans on the occasion of child-birth. Instantly a child is delivered, *Azan*, the customary prayer, is said at the right-hand side of the child. The *Azan*, or prayer, that is done in a much clearer voice audible to the ears of the born child, is of the following form :—" God is Great ! (said four times). I bear witness that there is no God but God (repeated twice). I bear witness that Mohammed is the Apostle of God (repeated twice). Come to prayers ! (said twice). Come to salvation ! (recited twice). God is Great ! (said twice). There is no Deity but the Deity !" (said only once) and the final call. This prayer being finished, another one of identical nature is done and said at the left side of the child. This second prayer, which is termed *Takbir*, contains wholly and exactly all the above quoted prayers, with only a concise addition to it of one or two words, to the following effect : "Hold thyself up firmly in prayer !" (recited twice). The *Azan* and the *Takbir*, it is believed by Moslems, are so done and read because the same do away with and keep aside the approach and haunt of the "devil" that ever lies in ambush and remains on the lookout to do or causing to do some wrong to the innocent, helpless child. The reading of this prayer, so believe Moslems, has the desired effect against the machinations and intended wrongs of the devil that is thus subdued, cowed down, and rendered powerless to do anything to the detriment and prejudice of the babe. The saying of such prayers, it is commonly held, exorcises at the same time all ghosts, spectres, or apparitions of any kind, usually common with babes, both circumstantially and locally. Of the devil, or Satan, it is believed by the generality of Islamitic doctors, that the same is at all moments ready to pillage and ruin the land and its children, whenever an opportunity presents itself ; but, say the doctors, it is all-powerful God alone that preserves His creation against all wrongs of the devil, who, it is said, has the power of depopulating and

---

[*] Vide the *Indian Daily News*, dated respectively, the 7th and the 8th of January, 1891, containing the authour's two different papers on this subject.

annihilating, in the twinkling of an eye, the entire world, if he finds a chance by any means. On the seventh day from the date of birth is celebrated with practicable means and power the rite known or called as *Akika*, when, as above said, the very expression imports, the babe's hair is cut off, and equal to the weight of the hair thus cut, gold or silver is distributed to paupers according to the pecuniary circumstance of the donor. A sumptuous meal is also served ; and a number of guests are entertained, all partaking except the parents of the babe. The meal so served is religiously required to consist of two kids in case of male babes, and one kid, of females. This limitation of the number of slaughter is not regarded by well-to-do persons, who are allowed to have as much slaughter of goats and kids as their means allow. The limit thus fixed is the minimum, and of the maximum no standard rule is made, but is left to the discretion of the persons keeping the ritual. The traditions of the Prophet have rendered it obligatory upon all believers in Islam having sufficient means for such celebration. As for the observance of the ceremony on the exact seventh or a certain appointed day reckoning from the birth, there is not a tittle of tradition in Islam to support or uphold this, inasmuch as the Prophet himself is said to have performed his own *Akika* in his advanced years. But it is lawful—because the Prophet has so enjoined—to hold the *Akika* once in life before paying the debt of nature. Goaded on with the keen instinct to celebrate it anyhow, modern Mussulmans have adopted for this celebration the seventh day after birth; and this has been pronounced lawful and commended by the doctors of Islam of the present century. On the occasion of a child-birth, Indian Mussulmans, much accustomed as they are to shows and gaieties, hold dancing, music, and other amusing attractions; none of which is allowable in any way in the Islamitic Book of Faith, which stands strictly opposed to all such novelties that were unknown in the Prophet's time, and to good Mussulmans of all ages from the holy Prophet downwards.

Akika, in the case of a boy, is shortly followed by

CIRCUMCISION,

which, though not mentioned at all in the *Koran*, is still held by Mohammedans to be an ancient Divine institution sanctioned by the

Prophet, and thereby confirmed in the religion of Islam. To the mind of Muslim doctors generally, circumcision owes its origin to the Patriarch Abraham. Yet some hold otherwise, and attribute it to Adam, who, as they say, was taught it by the Arch-angel Gabriel to satisfy an oath he had made to cut off the flesh which, after his well-known fall to earth from heaven, had rebelled against his spirit. From this narration some deduce an inference whereby a valid argument has been drawn for the universal obligation of circumcision. Others say that the ancient Arabs used to observe this rite for many ages before the advent of the Prophet, having probably learned it from *Ishmael*, who, in common with other tribes, practised the same. The Ishmaelites, it is said, used to circumcise their children, not on the eighth day, as is the custom of the Jews, but when about twelve or thirteen years old, at which age their father underwent that operation ; and the Mohammedans of this day imitate them so far as not to circumcise children before they are able, at least, distinctly to pronounce the profession of their Faith, " There is no God but God, and Mohammed is the Apostle of God." The age thus selected for the purpose now varies from six to sixteen, or thereabouts ; when they believe their children to be able to understand, or have a sufficient amount of judgment or knowledge of God, the Prophet, and of the Islamitish doctrine. Since some take circumcision, if done before the period, to be uncalled-for, and render it obligatory even when children have the requisite perceptive degree for bearing the operation; or when they begin growing to be subjected to the provisions of the Ecclesiastical Law of Faith. Many, however, circumcise their children immediately when they are born; but this practice is not frequent. The general usage of the modern Mussulmans is to circumcise their children any time below the age of ten years. The circumcision, though so obligatory, is withheld and dispensed with in cases of new converts to Islam, if advanced in years. Faith in God and belief in Alcoran, and obeisance to the Prophet, and to his successors and immediate followers, &c., are the only essentials for being a Mussulman. A person dying without observing the formality of circumcision, or things like this, can nowise be pronounced an infidel, for these usages, sanctioned as they are, emanate from the Prophet, whose only command

—not of God—is for the observance of circumcision. But since the Prophet's words are believed and taken to be the exact words of God, it is highly proper and expedient for all Mussulmans to observe to the fullest extent almost all the precepts and laws of the Holy Prophet. To deviate from and disobey in any way the Prophet, is to turn away from the Maker of all Being.

In the case of girls, Mussulmans have a similar ritual termed
GOSHWARAH,
which is done at the same time as boys are circumcised. Girls have their ears and noses pierced for the purpose of using rings and ornaments, such as Indian women are wont to wear.

Like *Akika*, in both these rites well-to-do Mussulmans, and especially those thirsting after *vanity and fame*, have all available merry-makings to please themselves and their surroundings. But all these, as already said, are anything but lawful and religious.

It remains only to add a few words upon the characteristics and personalities of Indian Mussulmans, who, in the event of a daughter's birth, consider themselves, like some Hindoos, accursed by Heaven, and think themselves greatly fortunate in having sons. Daughters, they say, only take away to others, when married, the valuables and treasures of the parental stock; sons add to the accumulated stores by the sweat of their brow, and afford means of comfort and pleasure to their parents. Girls they love very little, and always regard them as the property of others ; and consequently they do not set their hearts on them. Hence, one having a multiplicity of girls laments his hard lot and considers himself as the *accursed, discarded* of God. Such base and foolish views preponderate only amongst ignorant Mussulmans. The lettered class firmly object to these stupid ideas being entertained by a believer in Islam. But since the proportion of educated persons is in a very small minority, and illiterate ones comprise the majority of such thinkers, it may be taken as the universal notion of the Mussulmans inhabiting the country. In labouring under such a false thought, Mussulmans of the soil seem to have aped and copied, in its entirety and fullness, all that is now universally believed and done by Hindoos, whom we daily

see vituperating, through the journals of the time, the difficulties which
a poor Hindoo suffers in disposing of his maiden girls. As the Hindoo
girl question is now the theme of controversy in the Press, it would
be idle to enter into the topic at great length. Enlisting, as we do,
our sympathies alike both for the Hindoo and Mussulman girls, it only
remains to be exposed and propounded to the public eye what Islam
allows and ordains for such a ridiculous belief. It only needs the example
of the Prophet himself to show that Islam and its doctrinal faith stand
compactly averse to such foolish ideas. The Prophet, who himself loved
his daughter the most, has enjoined all his adherents to caress alike
all their children of either sex, and to make no distintion whatever in the
treatment of them. The glowing and eloquent words of the Prophet on
this matter, are as follows :—" Cursed are those who dislike and kick the
heavenly gift of offspring by offering accusations, and denunciations,
and evincing dissatisfaction against the sex and number of one's issue."
Such reluctance or discontent, so goes tradition, vitiates faith and causes
blaspheming to exist on the side of such wrong-thinking disclaimers and
dissenters. There is, however, a matter of great solace and rejoicing for
Mohammedans, to find that their Prophet's views are also fully shared by
all Europeans, who on the occurrence of a daugter's birth take as much
pride and pleasure as their Prophet took, and all good Mussulmans do
take still. In England and other countries there is a sort of Lord-
Mayor's day on the birth of daughters. Rationally, too, it is unfeeling
and unpleasant to hold two altogether different notions on the birth of
one's own children of separate sexes, and thus debase the feelings and
affections implanted in men by Nature.

THE MOHURRUM.*

The Moburrum, which for hundreds of years back has been going on with great *eclat* in Moslem families, is in remembrance of the martyrdom or death of Hassun and Hossein, grandsons of Mohammed the Prophet. This death or martyrdom, which has a specific name termed *Shahadut* in the phraseology of the Mohammedan doctrine, is the most memorable event in the pages of the annals of Islam, and is only second in importance to the Prophet's own obituary that occurred in 683 A. D., and is most reverently regarded by the Moslems of the world, since it fully bears testimony to the staunchest, unshaken belief of the heroes of the martyrdom who, in strict obeisance to God, manfully and very patiently suffered mortality for the preservation of Islam against tyrannies of certain led-astray Mussulmans who, like infidels, wanted to uproot and destroy it by the infusion and introduction into it of many innovations literally foreign to the essence and spirit of the religious standard. The history, founded on a strict relsable principle, and admitted unanimously by Moslems of all schools, runs to the effect that in 60 Hegira, long after the death of the Prophet and his four Califs, one Yazid, ruler of an extensive province in Arabia, with an intent to force his subjects to take him as head of their religion, claimed supremacy of the pulpit, and enjoined all believers of Islam in his domain to obey him as successor to the Caliphate. This was objected to by the entire bulk of Mussulmans of the time, who held these pretensions as blasphemy and infidelity : and openly opposed him in this act on the express plea that, in face of the then existing two grandsons of the Prophet, it was utterly irreligious and hellish to take others as the ecclesiastic head. Being thus baffled in his design, he resolved to behead the two holy grandsons under an impression that their end will clear away all obstacles in the way of gaining the object of his desires. Guided by this evil intention the wicked Yazid first threatened the two holiest beings to conform themselves to his obedience, and to dutifully recognise him as head of their religion.

---

* Vide the *Indian Daily News*, Monday, August 25, 1890, containing the author's paper *anent* the matter.

But the holy grandsons absolutely refused doing so on the specific ground that the intended desire on part of the pretender, if given effect to, was to give a death-blow to the Islamitic faith, which would materially suffer for this gratuitous, unwarranted claim of the pretender. This refusal went so far and high that men were hired by the profane Yazid for the arrest of the two dissenters, and when their apprehension could not be obtained, a large army was sent and arrayed against them to encompass their total end. The two *would-be* martyrs were then in Mecca, and thousands of entreaties by letters were made to them by the residents of Koofa, a place then under the subjugation of the devilish Yazid, inducing them to resort to Koofa to make the people their disciples; which they only outwardly evinced their desire to be so. The two holy personages, believing the Koofis, made their way to Koofa where they, on arrival, were struck to find a large army ready to battle with them. In the struggle that ensued Hossien, the second grandson of the Prophet, was murdered, and in such a cruel manner, that pen fails to amply narrate it. Hossein, on dying, was buried in a place called Kerbella, which to this day is worshipped generally by Mohammedans of all persuasions and by Shiahs particularly. The first grandson, Hasun, was poisoned by his own wife, Jada, who in collusion and concert with Yazid, and in idea of worldly gains that she coveted from him, so caused the end of her husband by venom administered by stealth seven times to him in his food. The death of these two martyrs finally closed the war which lasted full ten days, commencing from the 1st to the 10th day of Mohurrum. These ten days now form the subject of the anniversary all over the Mohammedan world, and are exclusively observed in mourning by every believer of Islam. The *taziah alum* and other rites, as observed during these ten days, are only in commemoration of the martyrdom; but these forms of worship are entirely disallowed for Mohammedans of the *Sunni*** school, and are only in

---

* *Sunni*, an Arabic word, is derived from "*Sunna*" meaning regulation. It is a belief common to the whole Muslim world that Mohammed, as regards all that he said or did, was supernaturally guided from on high; hence it follows that his words and actions constitute a divine rule of faith and practice; this is the doctrine which underlies the fabric of the *Sunni* creed with its

currency and force with the *Shiahs*.† The originality of these demonstrations is due to Timour the Great, and does not go beyond his time. *Shiahs* have these demonstrations to cherish and perpetuate the event-

---

145,000,000, of votaries. (For the beliefs and the *essentials* of the *Sunni* school see (1) *Bokhari*, (2) *Sahih-i-Muslim*, (3) *Sunnan-i-Abu-Daud*, (4) *Jami-i-Tirmizi*, (5) *Sunan-i-Nasai*, and (6) *Sunnan-i-Ibn-Maja*, the principal six treatises touching the faith of the *Sunnis* whose origin is exclusively due to these six *Sahihain* (or books) which are reckoned and believed by them as the only authourities next in importance to those of the *Koran* itself. (For English books on the creed, see, amongst numerous others, (1) Mr. Wollaston's "Half Hours with Mohammed," Chapter VI entitled the "Sects of Islam;" page 267 : and (2) George Sale's "English Koran" and his "Preliminary Discourse" on it; section 8, page 107.)

† *Shiahs*, who are next to *Sunnis* or *Sonnites*, are the second great division of the Muslim Faith, which, supplanting the religion founded by Zoroaster, who is generally supposed to have flourished from B. C. 521 to B. C. 485, has become the national doctrine of the Persian Monarchy and is now the religion of millions of people inhabiting India and other spheres of the globe. According to Mr. Blunt's account, the *Shiahs*, to this day, number 15,000,000, souls.

The only important points at issue between the rival *Sunnis* and *Shiahs*, excluding other minor matters, are these :—That *Shiahs*, who profess to be strict adherents or followers of Huzrut Ali, the fourth and last successor or Caliph of the Prophet, reject the first three Califs (Huzruts Abu Bakar, Umar, and Usman), and believe that Huzrut Ali's descendants, from Huzrut Imam Hasun to Huzrut Imam Mehdi, were Prophet's true successors, and as such raised far above all other Muslims as regards character, position, and dignity : while, *Sunnis*, who thoroughly believe in all the dignities and qualifications which these holy personages were naturally possessed of, admit the successions in order of all the four Caliphs to Ali downwards and give preference to them only as to matters relating to their personal characteristics. The *Shiahs*, on the other hand, though believe in the first three Caliphs but reject them so far as the Caliphate is concerned. In fine, contests and differences between these two rival sects are only about matters relating to the merits or demerits of certain individuals succeeding to the Caliphate. To an enlightened, honest, and just observer, both are Moslems and followers of one and the same prophet. (For English writings on the *Shiahs*, see, among others, *(a)* Wollaston's aforesaid book, page 289 ; and *(b)* Sale's above work, page 124.)

ful ceremony, while *Sunnis* spend these ten days in fasting, alms-giving, prayers, &c. The object for which *Yazid* undertook the war was totally frustrated; since after the mournful occurrence, the whole universe arose against him: and when about to take revenge of him, he died of a natural death. Mussulmans of all schools believe *in toto* in the martyrdom, and observe it in the form and manner as allowed in their respective religions. The anniversary has now become so popular amongst diverse nationalities that even Hindoos, Christians, and Jews observe it in some way or other.

The martyrdom, as above said, actually happened on the 10th of Mohurrum in the year of 61 of the Hegira, corresponding with 19th October 680 A. D., and this tenth day of Mohurrum, which is commonly called "Yom-i-Ashoora" is now held sacred on many accounts; because it is believed to be the day on which the first meeting of Adam and Eve took place after they were cast out of Paradise; and that on which Noah went out from the ark: also, because several other great events are said to have happened on this day; and because the ancient Arabs, before the time of the Prophet, observed it by fasting. But what, in the opinion of most modern Moslems, and especially the Persians, confers the greatest sanctity on the day of Ashoora, is the fact of its being that on which Hossein, the Prophet's second grandson, was, as here said, slain a martyr, at the battle of the plain of Kerbella. Many Moslems fast on this day, and some also on the day preceeding.

Mr. Edward William Lane, in his "Account of the manners and customs of the Modern Egyptians," says of a particular meal which is prepared on this day by the Egyptians; and which, really unknown as it is to most Indian Mussulmans, is worth reproduction here. Speaking of the festivities observed by the Egyptians on this Ashoora day he says :—" On my paying a visit to a friend, a little before noon, a dish, which it is the custom of the people of Cairo to prepare on the day of Ashoora, was set before me. It is called "Haboob;" and is prepared with wheat, steeped in water for two or three days, then freed from the husks, boiled, and sweetened over the fire with honey or treacle : or it is composed of rice instead of wheat : generally, nuts, almonds, raisins, &c., are added to it. In most houses this dish is prepared, or sweetmeats of various kinds are procured or made, in accordance with one of the traditions of the Prophet; which is—" Whoso giveth plenty to his household on the day of Ashoora, God will bestow plenty upon him throughout the remainder of the year."

In bringing forward this tradition as the basis of his argument for supporting the existence of the so-called dish, Mr. Lane seems to have literally ignored and overlooked some indisputable well-established points in connection therewith. He ought to have at least given a deliberate thought to the subject before enlarging upon it, and ought to have noticed, amongst numerous others, the following particular matters :—

Hossein's martyrdom or death did occur neither in the time of the Prophet, nor during the successive periods of his four Caliphs, the pillars of Islam. It happened long after the death of these personages, and, consequently, none of them ever had the least opportunity of personally observing a ritual like this, or of taking part of it in any way. The observance of such a rite forms nowise a subject of the *essentials* sanctioned and authorised by the Koran and the Mohamedan Ecclesiastical Law of Faith; and the Prophet and his four Caliphs, the real founders of Islamism, have nowhere laid down any rules or enjoined their followers for keeping the celebration of the kind though it is admittedly true that the holy Prophet had in his lifetime predicted the *would-be murder of Hossein* : but this prognostication itself does neither pave the way for the celebration nor does it tend to authourise the sanctity of the ritualism, the subject matter of Mr. Lane's elaborate writing on it. Hence, the tradition, which he so professes to rely upon, is a pure fiction.

Quot homines, tot sententiæ.

Before we leave the *Mohurrum* and turn to another subject, we draw attention of our readers to the author's following letter which appeared some years ago in the well-known Calcutta Journal, the *Statesman.* The letter, which forms the theme of a serious hot discussion that arose long ago on the *Mohurrum* question between the author and his personal esteemed friend, the late lamented Robert Knight, Editor of the said journal on one side ; and the then varieties of debaters or haranguers on the other, will speak for itself :—

THE MOHURRUM QUESTION.*

TO THE EDITOR.

SIR,—A letter† headed as above, appears in your yesterday's issue in which the writer, who signs himself MIRZA, remarks as follows :—

" You say that the Koran gives the demonstrations no sanction whatever.‡ The simplest answer to this, would be that it does nowhere forbid such demonstrations, as are founded on religious grounds, with the confirmation of what we call the Khali-fat-ul-Allah (the Viceroy of God) and his deputies—the Mujtahdin and Ulamas."

With your permission, I would put the following questions to MIRZA, which I hope he will frankly answer :—

(1) Have these annual demonstrations ever received the sanction of the Khalifas (Caliphs), and if so, where is the authority to this effect?

(2) Have the Khalifas, or any of them, ever personally observed these commemorations ?

(3) Has any ceremony, simply sanctioned and not followed by the Khalifas themselves, ever had the force of precept or law? Cite the instance, if there be any.

For my own part, my belief is that no such customs as these *Mohurrum* processions by Indian Mussulmans, have ever received the sanction of the Khalifs, Mujtahdin, or Ulamas, and that it is a false theory to suppose otherwise. These pillars of Islam have allowed the following practices to be observed during the ten days of *Mohurrum* :—

(a) To fast; (b) to offer prayers, day and night, to the martyr Hossain and his fellow-sufferers ; (c) to give charity to the poor and needy in their name ; (d) to weep and mourn over their cruel martyr-

* See the *Statesman and Friend of India*, Friday, November 5, 1886.
† For this letter also see *Ibid.*
‡ For his editorial and other writings on the *Mohurrum* see *ibidem.*

dom; (c) to abstain during these days from pleasures, and to behave
as one does when bereaved of dear parents or near relatives in the
extent of our sorrow. These are the only prescriptions of Islam to be
found in every book of faith. Even these do not command strict
observance, but are left to the free will of the observants, and are not
of religious importance, such as the daily prayers, the *Ramzan*
fastings, and other ceremonies, &c. If, as Mussulmans, we do not
observe these precepts, we have no faith and no religion, their non-
observance being a sin against the meaning and spirit of Alkoran, and
opposed to the command and will of God and of the prophet Mohammed (upon whom be the peace and mercy of God). In addition to
these indispensable commands, if we observe *Mohurrum* in such ways
as above stated, they will be virtuous and good deeds, but nothing
more, as we are in no way answerable before God for non-observance
of the *Mohurrum*. Formalities are not a leading principle of Islam,
and *tazias* and *alums* are not the best means of expressing our sorrow.
The holy and pious of yore, who were the strictest celebrants of
Mohurrum, did never practise these things, nor did they ever dream of
doing so. It is untrue therefore to say, that these things owe their
origin to the leaders of Islam. No one who has competent knowledge of the subject will deny that these demonstrations are of modern
date. Islam forbids all shows and demonstrations, and why there
should be special privilege as regards *tazias* and *alums* is difficult to
understand. Would their suppression cause any change in our religious system? Certainly not. But there is no need for Government
interfering in such matters. The enlightened men among the Mohammedans themselves, should endeavour to do away with such demonstrations, preserving only what is of value in their observance. These
demonstrations have here become more a theme of play-acting and
pleasure, instead of being an annual occasion of lamentation and
mourning. Mirza will find few enlightened Mohammedans to support
him when he so vigorously speaks in favour of them.

 P. S.—When agitation is made for the suppression of these
Mohurrum demonstrations, the same rule should be applied to the *Ram-
lila* demonstrations, which are as outrageous as those in question.

THE "MILAD."*

The Mohammedan month, styled the *Rabiul-awul*, or first spring, is the time of the birth of the holy Prophet Mohammed, who, in accordance with the Islamitic tradition, was born on a Monday, and on the 12th of the month which is the 3rd month of the Moslem year. The birth, which occurred at early dawn, is, according to religious dogma, concerned with many historical striking and superhuman incidents which came to light along with the birth, as indicative of the eventful occurrence, prognosticating the advent into the world of Mohammed, the last of the hundreds of Prophets who successively flourished in the world with God's holy command to keep the creation safe and properly guarded from the wickedness and the bad insinuations of the devil, the notorious Satan whose constant pursuit, as say the religious books, is to lead astray men from the good to the bad path; and thus to render them sinful and obnoxious before the all-powerful God. Of the varieties of fundamental holy principles that Mohammed and all his predecessors had to teach, and for which they had especially revealed themselves, the only obligatory and essential precepts had been three, *viz.*—first, Unitarianism, or Deism; second, the obedience to the Prophets and belief in them; and third, total abstinence from idolatry and from worshipping any except God.

Of the numerous occurrences of note that were presented to the eye of the world on the day Mohammed the Prophet first stepped into the universe from his parents, the holy Abdullah and Bibi Amina, on all of whom be the peace, mercy, and love of God, were (1) that all the then idols of the world whom infidels used to worship as their Gods had their heads bent downwards by themselves, as expressive of the fact that idolatry, which long before had infected and polluted the living world, would soon be annihilated by the Prophet's appearance; (2) that the great fire of Persia which infidels worshipped, and had illuminated and kept for so many thousand years, extinguished itself, as indicative, of the total destruction of *fire-worship* in the Prophet's

---

* (Vide the *Indian Daily News*, Saturday, October 18, 1890, containing the authour's lecture on the subject.)

time; and (3) that the 14 minarets of the palace of the then Great King of Persia, Nosherawan, fell by themselves, as showing the end of the King's family, and the substitution thereof of the 14 future other Kings from his descent. The religious books of Islam teem with millions of miracles and wonderful things, brought to light both at the time of the Prophet's birth and in his lifetime, when he revealed himself as Prophet, and expounded all the hidden secrets, words, and commands of God.

The Prophet's birth, which came with such pomp and show, is now the theme of the annual celebration amongst Mahommedans of all persuasions and schools. The ritual, which generally lasts the first two weeks of the *Rabiul-awul* month, has now become so conspicuously popular by its importance that true Mussulmans keep the observance throughout the year whenever they possibly can. This rite has a specific name termed *"Milad,"* or *" Moloud-i-Sharif,"* meaning thereby the Prophet's sacred birth celebration; and in this jovial meeting or merry-making party hundreds of Mohammedans of all denominations unite and assemble to hear books or passages from the Koran read or recited by readers, whose only duty it is to read over to their audience the poems and prose works, and all sorts of available writings, works dealing exclusively with the Prophet's personal virtues and qualities, his birth, and all the events attending it ; and also dealing with his childhood and manhood, together with all the surrounding weighty accidents that happened in the course of his life.

Of many noticeable matters the most important of all is the *Miraj* night, when the Prophet, in the twinkling of an eye, is said to have travelled over all parts of the skies, and to have seen and met the Omnipotent, Omnipresent, and Omniscient God. It is in this night that the Prophet resorted from Mecca to Jerusalem, or *baitul-mokud-dus*, the mausoleum of the former Prophets, where Mohammed is said to have met the Prophets who lived there, and to have led them in a prayer which was done literally to obtain for him the leadership of and superiority over all his predecessors. It was in that very night that he attained salvation for his followers, and the ordinary forms of prayers now in practice were ordained and prescribed by Nature for his believers and dependents.

These are the objects and the customary rites and usages which are so reverently observed by Moslems of the universe in this month especially, but also in other months of the year.

THE FATEHA-YAZDAHUM.*

This is a festive celebration observed annually by Mohammedans of the *Sunni* persuasion, on the eleventh of the fourth Mussulman month, termed *Rabius-sani*, which is said to be the date of the birth of their spiritual leader, Huzrut Syed Mohiuddin Abdul Kadir, of Ghilan, the greatest of all the Moslem saints —upon whom ever be the love, peace, and mercy of God.

This birth-day the Mohammedans celebrate in the same manner as they do in observing the Prophet's birth-day† of the *Rabbi-ul-awul* month; and as on that occasion, they even here spend this day in offering prayers to the departed soul of the saint, in giving charity to mendicants in his name and memory; reading and reciting books and passages dealing with the personalities, excellent virtues, and super-human powers of the saint; recalling the noteworthy incidents touching his birth, together with such anecdotes and weighty events as happened in the course of his life. This Huzrut is one of the near collateral descendants in the eleventh pedigree of the holy Hasun and Hossein, grandsons of the Prophet ; and by his pre-eminence and superiority in miracles, is the recognised head and master of all the Moslem saints, past and future. As the Prophet is believed to be the head of all his predecessors, so this Huzrut is thought to be chief of all *dervishes* (religious mendicants), who (so goes the general impression) cannot attain the virtues *sine quâ non* for saints unless, or until, they conform themselves to his modes of life, and to his express or implied obedience. Without this obeisance and homage, none, it is said, can be admitted to the class or range of *dervishes ;* since, as the Father of saints, he is recognised as the originator of the *dervish* creed or flock. He is said to have been very highly commended for his great virtues and qualities by the Prophet himself, who is reported to have remarked of him,— "*Mohiuddin*, or reviver of decayed Islam, will surpass all saints in piety and godly devotions, and all saints will especially be under him.

---

* (Vide the *Indian Daily News*, Wednesday, November 26, 1890, containing a paper on this by the author).

† See chapter entitled the "*Millad*" page 13.

He who dissents from or disobeys him will be done for permanently ; and the one who takes him as his head or chief will alone attain the rank of the saints, since he, as my descendant and successor, will revive and reform, on a truly solid basis, Islamism, when in its waning state in after ages long behind me; and by his remarkable reforms and improvements, he will be subsequently named *Mohiuddin.*"

Among Mussulmans it is a prevalent belief that Mohiuddin alone would have become a prophet, had there been any more prophet after Mohammed, the last of all the thousands of prophets. Abdul Kadir Mohiuddin, in the Hindustani phraseology, is called by the bulk of Indian Mussulmans as *burrapir*, or saint-in-chief. Modern Mohammedans divide Islam into four spiritual congregations, of which the first is the one founded by Syed Mohiuddin Abdul Kadir of Ghilan, and termed " Kadri ;" and three other such sects as were founded by three different saints who consecutively succeeded Al-kadir, are respectively called (2)* *Chishti,* (3)† *Nukhsbundia,* and (4) *Saharwardia.*

Mohiuddin's disciples extol him almost to the skies; but the divided unrebuttable view of the generality of good pious Mussulmans is that, in rank, position and virtues, he stands next to the Prophet, his four holy Caliphs, and to those ancestors from whom *Mohiuddin* descends. The celebration of the subject of this article, and the forms and manner of worship which the present Indian and other foreign Mussulmans observe and do, receive no sanction and authority whatever from the Holy Koran; nor have the same ever been licensed or enjoined by the Prophet and his Caliphs, or his immediate and subsequent followers. But, on the other hand, these observances are in the pure Islamitic sense, thoroughly *biddut*, or unlawful, and consequently punishable by God. *Biddut*, in religion, means an utter innovation, and the one never done or observed by the Prophet or his Caliphs, or immediate followers and successors. Islam only requires men to obey God, the

* This is named after its founder, Huzrut Khajah Moinuddin Chishti who lies buried in Ajmore.

† This and the next one " Saharwardia," are founded by the saints named respectively (1) Huzrut Moulana Syed Bahauddin Nukhshbund and (2) Huzrut Shaikh Shahabuddin Saharwardi.

Prophet, and the Caliphs, and his successors. Such obedience is confined wholly to the dictates of the *Koran* and to what the Prophet has decreed and ordained for his follower's actions in the world.

It is only illiterate, benighted Mussulmans that make it their special duty to give effect to such useless festivals, and instead of these bootless observances, had they given themselves up more to the *essentials* of the Islamitic doctrine, they would doubtless have acquired some substantial reward in the world to come. Among Mussulmans there is a class of loafers who style themselves as *fakirs* or *pirs* and make thousands of ignorant poor Mussulmans their *morids*, or disciples ; and it is only such self-interested *pirs* who make, and have made, these merry-makings the source of their earnings and livings, by getting so many led-astray Mussulmans to join in the performance of such ritual upon which they mainly subsist.

THE "SHUB-I-BARAT."*

" SHUB-I-BARAT," which is a compound Persian word, is formed
of the two different terms, *shub* and *barat*, the former of which means
night, and the latter a *cheque*, or *paper*, for the realisation or grant of
certain accumulated sums of money, or eatables, from some hidden
store or treasury. Religiously, it signifies a portion or share allotted
to, or bestowed on, mankind by Providence. This *night* of *share*,
which falls on the 15th of the Mohammedan eighth month, called
Shaban, means to indicate the one specific night in which God sends
forth from heaven through His holy angels, the prescribed yearly portion of living or food for His creation in the world. In this special
night are, so says religion, fixed and decreed by Nature,—(a) The
amount or share of living which each of mankind has to receive in the
year round ; (b) the date of a person's death within the year, and (c)
the standard of all the actions, good or bad, which people have to do
or commit in the year, commencing from the appearance of the night
in question. These matters, so hold and assert doctors of divinity,
are so particularly and fully dealt with by God on that very night,
that the standards and the rules framed and settled therein can in no
wise be shaken or departed from ; and that all such prescribed ordi-
nations must needs have their thorough fulfilment and completion,
without let or hindrance, within the time specified by God for their
accomplishment. In this night, angels descend to the earth and resort to and meet every being, distributing and giving to all of them
what God so provides, rules, and ordains for His creation's necessaries
of life, together with their ultimate fate and eventual circumstances
and worldy connections and movements all the year round. Such,
say doctors, is the Providential work done or observed every year ;
and this continues as times roll and fleet away, and lasts or remains
in force till one's fate becomes finally doomed, or sealed.

This night, which happens once annually, for disposing and set-
tling all the events of the ensuing year with respect to life and death
and the other surroundings and affairs, is only next in importance to

---

* Vide the *Indian Daily News*, Tuesday, December 9, 1890, containing
a portion of the authour's present article on the subject.

one other night, styled, *Shub-i-Kadar*, which, signifying, as it really does, *power*, and *honour* or *dignity*, and also the *Divine decree*, excels and surpasses all other nights in the year, and which, as Moslem doctors affirm, takes place in one of the ten last nights of *Ramadan*, and, as is commonly believed, on the seventh of these nights, reckoning backwards : by which, as says Jalla-ud-din, a doctor of great note and credit, it is meant that it falls between the twenty-third and twenty-fourth days of the Ramadan month. In the *Shub-i-barat* night which, after the above *Kadar*, is believed by Mussulmans to be a very holy and dignified one, the *Koran* (so go the traditions) was commanded by God to be sent down from His Holy Throne, entitled *Loh-i-Mahfooz*, in the seventh-highest heaven, to *Baitul izzaut*, a heavenly abode in the first lowest sky. The holy Koran was actually first revealed to the living world in the *Kadar* night of the *Ramadan* month ; yet it much also owes to the *Shub-i-barat* night, when *it* (the Koran) *began* to descend from the skies. Like *Kadar* the *Barat* is a good and auspicious night for prayers, and in both these nights prayers are readily listened to ; and in case of a true penitent past sins are pardoned and expunged by the All-powerful God, who, in these nights, augments and stretches forth evenly to all beings His boundless tender blessings and mercies. On all true Mussulmans it perforce devolves to spend these nights specially in prayers, and to do and cause to be done all possible virtuous deeds for their future good. Any one spending otherwise these holy ominous nights incurs—so says religion—a great heavenly displeasure ; and bitterly incenses God against himself.

The Sadur (or Lote-tree) of Paradise, which is more commonly called Shujratul-Muntaha (or the Tree of the * Extremity), probably for several reasons, but chiefly (as is generally supposed) because it is said to be at the extremity, or on the most elevated spot, in Paradise, is believed by Muslims to have as many leaves as there are living human beings in the world ; and the leaves are said to be inscribed

* In the Commentary of the Jalalain, "Shujratul-Muntaha," or the Lote-tree of the Extremity, is interpreted as signifying "The Lote-tree beyond which neither angels nor others can pass."

with the names of all those beings ; each leaf bearing the name of one person, and that of his father and mother. This tree, Moslems believe, is shaken in the *Shub-i-barat* night, a little after sunset ; and when a person is destined to die in the ensuing year, his leaf, upon which his name is so written, falls on this occasion : if he be to die very soon, his leaf is almost wholly withered, a very small portion only remaining green: if he be to die later on in the year, a larger portion remains green: according to the time he has yet to live, so is the proportion of the part of the leaf yet green. This, therefore, is a very awful night to the serious and considerate Muslims; who, accordingly, observe it with solemnity and earnest prayer. The following, among several others, is a specimen of the special prayers used by pious Mussulmans on this auspicious occasion:—" O God ! O Thou Gracious ! and who art not an object of grace ! O Thou Lord of Dignity and Honour, and of Beneficence and Favour ! There is no deity but Thou, the Support of those who seek to Thee for refuge, and the Helper of those who have recourse to Thee for help, and the Trust of those who fear ; O God, if Thou hast recorded me in thy abode, upon the 'Original of the * Book,' miserable, or unfortunate, or scanted in my sustenance, cancel, O God, of thy goodness, my misery, and misfortune, and scanty allowance of sustenance, and confirm me in thy abode, upon the Original of the Book, as happy, and provided for, and directed to good : for Thou hast said (and thy saying is perfectly true) in thy Book revealed by the tongue of thy commissioned Prophet, 'God will confirm and cancel what He pleases ; and with Him alone is the Original of the Book.' † O my God ! by the very great revelation (which is made) in this night ‡ of the middle of the month

---

* By this, it is here commonly understood and believed to be "The Preserved Tablet of the seventh heaven, which is called Loh-i-Mahfooz," and on which are said to be written the original of the Koran, and all decrees of God. It is further said that the "Original" (or, literally, the "Mother") " of the Book" is God's knowledge, or prescience.

† See *Koran*, Chapter 13, entitled, Thunder, verse 39.

‡ Arabic term for this Night is "*Lailatun-Nuf-min-Shaban*" which also means the very thing. This night, which actually is the night of the fifteenth of the Shaban month, means the night preceding the fifteenth day of the month.

of Shaban the honoured, 'in which every determined decree is dispensed*
and confirmed,' remove from me whatever affliction I know, and what
I know not, and what Thou best knowest; for Thou art the most
Mighty, the most Bountiful. And favour, O God, our Lord Mohammed, the Illiterate † Prophet, and his Family and Companions, and
preserve them." Amen ! Amen ! Amen !

During the *Shub-i-barat* festival Moslems of the day—especially
of India—have demonstrations consisting of fire-works, illumination,
and all other fancy playthings for their pleasure; and they observe
this ritual just in the same way that Hindoos do their *Dewali* ceremonial. But none of these subjects which modern Moslems take to
heart on the occasion of the rite, is in any way authorised and sanctioned by the *Koran*; nor has the same ever received direct or indirect
approval by the Prophet, his Caliphs, successors, and immediate
followers. This, like the *Yazdahoom-Fateha* noticed ‡ in the previous
Chapter, is a pure innovation and severely punishable by God, and is
the concocted and self-invented action of benighted Mussulmans.

To this class of celebration also belongs the festival named
Akhiri-chahar-shumbah, or last Wednesday of the Mohammedan
second month, called *Safar*, which is said to have been the time and
date of the Prophet's recovery from a severe illness, and which most

---

* See *Koran*, Chapter 45, verse 3. Opinions of Doctors of Divinity
vary as to the so-called "dispensation" and some attribute this to the Night
of Alkadur.

† It is admittedly true that the Prophet was illiterate, and this fact is
also corroborated by God's own words in the Koran in its Chapter, entitled,
Al-Araf; but this, in itself, is an evident proof of his divine mission; and a
good reasonable ground for Non-Mussulmans to hold and affirm that the writings produced by the Prophet as direct revelations from God, could nowise
be a forgery of his own; because it was utterly impossible for a person like
him, who could neither write nor read, to be able to compose a book of such
excellent doctrine, and in so unequally elegant a style. This illiteracy, as the
only best evidence of his being inspired, totally nullifies and vitiates all the
gratuitous false accusations which Anti-Mussulmans wrongly and bigotedly
bring against the Prophet and charge him with being an impostor.

‡ See page 16.

ignorant Mussulmans keep with great veneration and strictness. They consider it their duty to celebrate it with extravagant pomp or great special preparation. On this event they bathe, and use some amulets as a protection against evils or impending perils and troubles. But all these are in no way established or substantiated by any religious doctrinal authority or principle; and hence the same is anything but good and lawful, and ought, consequently, to be abandoned once for all by true Mussulmans on the path to religion and faith. Mussulmans who avow and profess to be disciples of some holy saints, and style themselves *Kadris, Hanifis*, &c., alone betake themselves to these invented and literally unfounded practices; and thus have already rendered, and are daily making Islamism and its beauties detestable to the eyes of the civilised race, by these their evil and pernicious pursuits, which it is high time for the rising and enlightened generation to put a stop to, and by so doing to remove the impediments that lamentably stand in the way of the future improvement and development of their fallen illiterate co-religionists. The high sounding titles of the tribe describing themselves as *Kadris, Hanifis*, &c., have no authority from the Koran for assuming these epithets, nor has the Prophet so over allowed them to be and to do. In Islam it is *de facto* indispensable for every one to strictly and most rigidly conform himself to naught save and except to what has been enjoined and ordained by Nature and His Viceroy, the Prophet; and every thing going against their express commands and directions, amounts to sins abominable and accountable to the Creator in the age to come. Being a true, pious Mussulman, does in no way, confine to one's being a *Kadri* or *Hanifi*; but materially rests with one's action in entire consonance and accordance with the commandments and the prescribed rules and directions of the Mohammedan ecclesiastical law. During the *Shub-i-barat* it is lawful to offer prayers for the salvation and the good of the spirits of the departed kinsmen and acquaintances, and to give away alms in their memory and name. In this night, as above said, God bends and inclines to earth and its beings, and mercifully grants to all what they demand of and want from Him, and graciously absolves repentants of their sins.

Shaban is, in a manner, a prepartion for *Ramadan*, or fasting, which follows next to it, and is in one strict sense a happy intelligence to believers in Islam for the coming *Ramadan*, a high Moslem anniversary.

THE RAMAZAN.[*]

The *Ramazan*, which is observed by Mussulmans all over the world with more or less strictness, in accordance with the precepts of the Koran, is the ninth month of the Mohammedan year, and the word is derived from *ramz* to burn, the month being so called because it is supposed to burn away the sins of men.

Among the earliest, if not the first, revelation which Mohammed presented to his followers in the Koran is the " Revelation of the Cow," so called from a vision of a heifer which the Prophet interpreted. This revelation was made to him at Mecca and at Medina, and it sets forth in graceful and flowing language directions to the pious to observe the faith with prayer, including ablution, fasting, alms, and pilgrimage. In its 286 verses of such general import are to be found several which deal with the question of fasting during the month of *Ramazan* or the month of fasting. The Mohammedan community engage in the exercise of this form of devotion, which was ushered in with the month, and which continued for thirty days, as is commanded in the Koran, where it is written—" Oh, true believers, a fast is ordained to you, as it was ordained before you, that ye may fear God: the month of *Ramazan* shall ye fast, in which the Koran was sent down from heaven." This month was called "the month of wine" by the old Arab pagans, during which they drank to excess, but the Prophet changed it into the month of fasting. A Moslem writer says : " Prayer leads us half way to God ; fasting conveys us to His threshold ; but alms conduct us into His presence." The importance of fasting is thus considered a virtue second only to alms-giving, which, with denunciations on the head of the infidel, form two of the subjects most elaborated on in the Koran. A Mohammedan will never refuse alms to a beggar, and every keeper of that faith thinks it as necessary to have his bag of the smallest money coined for distribution in charity, as he does to have his stock-in-trade.

It was a custom among the ancient Arabs to observe four months in the year as sacred, during which they held it unlawful to wage war, unfastened their spears, and ceased from incursions and other hostilities. During those months, whoever was in fear of his enemy lived in peaceful security ; so that if a man met the murderer of his father or his brother, he durst not offer him any violence. The months so held sacred by the Arabs were *Mohurrum, Rajab, Zikad,* and *Zilhij* ; the first, the seventh, the eleventh, and the twelfth in the year. *Zilhij* being the month wherein they performed the pilgrimage to Mecca, not only that month, but also the preceding and the following months, were for that reason kept inviolable, that every one might safely and without molestation pass and repass to and from the holy city. *Rajab* is said to have been then more strictly observed than any of the other three, because in that month the pagan Arabs used to fast. *Ramazan,* which was afterwards set apart by Mohammed for the same purpose, was, as just above said, in the earlier history of Mohammedanism spent in drinking and riotious living. By reason of the profound peace and security enjoyed in this month, one part of the provisions brought by the caravans of purveyors annually sent out by the Koresh tribe for the supply of Mecca* was distributed among the people, the other part being, for the like reason, distributed at the place of pilgrimage. The observance of the aforesaid months seemed so reasonable to Mohammed, that it met with his unqualified approval, and it was accordingly confirmed and enforced by several passages† of the Koran, which forbid the waging of war during those months against such as acknowledge them to be sacred, but grant the Faithful at the same time full permission to attack those who make no such acknowledgment.

Fasting, or what is called *Ramazan,* is, among the various main practices of Mussulmans, the third point of their religion—duty of such great moment, that Mohammed used to say it was " the gate of religion," and that " the odour of the mouth of him who fasteth is more grateful to God than that of musk;" while Imam Gizah, one of the prominent doctors of the Islamitic faith, reckons fasting " one-fourth

---

* See *Koran,* Chapter 106, entitled *Koresh.*

† See *Koran,* Chapters 9, 2, and 4.

part of the faith." The reason why the month of *Ramazan* was selected for this purpose was, as already stated, that on that month the Koran was sent down from Heaven.

It is, moreover, expressly admitted by all Doctors of the Islamitic faith and authoritatively laid down in almost all the religious works of renowned spiritual preceptors of the Moslem doctrines, that impious and sinful Mussulmans, when they die and are buried, suffer till doom's day every sort of privation and difficulties for the wrongs and vices they have committed in life. Such miseries they undergo for the full eleven months of the year save and except during the holy month of *Ramazan*, when their sufferings and trials cease, from the day the moon of the month appears till its close on the first day of *Shawal* succeeding the "*Ramazan*." Another tradition is that from the first day of the "*Ramazan*," to its termination, the gates of Heaven are laid open to the world and those of hell literally shut against it; meaning thereby that during the sacred month, the world and its creatures experience varieties of good, peace and comforts.

According to Mohammedan divines, there are three degrees of fasting : (1) the restraining of the appetite and passions ; (2) the restraining of the different members of the body, such as the ears, eyes, tongue, hands, feet, and other members, from sin ; and (3) the spiritual fasting or the contemplation of God. The Mohammedans are obliged, by the express command of the Koran, to fast the whole month of *Ramazan*, from the first appearance of the new moon till its reappearance the next month during the whole of this time they are supposed to abstain from eating, drinking, and licentiousness, from daybreak till nightfall or sunset. And this injunction they observe so strictly that while they fast they suffer nothing to enter their mouths, or any polluted thing to touch their bodies, esteeming the fast broken if they smell perfumes, or bathe, or even swallow their spittle ; some being so cautious that they will not open their mouths to speak, lest they should breathe the air too freely. The fast is also deemed void if a man kisses or touches a woman, or if he expectorates designedly. But after sunset they are permitted to refresh themselves, and to eat and rink and enjoy the company of their wives till daybreak ; though the nore rigid begin the fast again at midnight.

Pious Mussulmans spend the whole of the *Ramazan* in saying prayers or in doing some virtuous deed. To commit or to be implicated in any crime during the month is to them an unpardonable sin ; and it is not unusual to see confirmed drunkards become at this sacred season sober men. *Ramazan* is considered so purifying and important a festival that those who throughout the year never say a prayer or do any act of religious worship devote the whole of the month to prayers and religious duties as an atonement for their past sins, and as the safest way to heaven, which, as they say, is reserved only for men of virtue. From morning dawn, or three o'clock A. M. till the appearance of the stars at night, which is generally seven o'clock in the evening, all good Mussulmans abstain from everything which it is supposed is likely to break their fast, and spend the day in reading the Koran, saying their prayers, or in doing other acts of piety. Their first meal, with which they break their fast in the evening, consists as a rule of all manner of vegetables and fruits. The second meal, which follows shortly after the first one, consists of bread, meat, boiled rice or *pilao* and any other soild food which they may like to take. These two are the principal meals they have in *Ramazan*. At 3 o'clock in the night, *i. e.*, some hours before sunrise, they drink milk or take some light refreshment as a prevention against thirst during the day. From the fast of *Ramazan* none, so goes tradition or precept, are excused, except travellers and sick persons (under which last denomination the doctors include all whose health would manifestly be injured by their keeping the fast, such as women with child, or women nursing, superannuated persons, and young children) ; but even these are obliged as soon as the objections mentioned cease to fast an equal number of days at any other time of the year, and breaking the fast can only be expiated by alms-giving.

Fasting, it is held and maintained by doctors of Islam, is dearly loved by God because it coincides with the numerous qualities of Him who does not eat and drink. Those who do not observe the *Ramazan* will never be permitted to enter at the gate of heaven called " *ruiyan* " through which will be admitted only those who have regularly observed the holy fasting ; and that, according to another tradition save the one just above described, such defaulters, if they intend to atone for their past neglect, shall have to fast sixty days for each day so lost, and to daily feed sixty paupers till the last day of *Ramazan*. The above detailed reasonable causes only as sickness, superannuation, etc., entitle people to exemption according to religion. But in that case even they must give alms according to their means or must as already said fast an equal number of days at any other time of the year. Mohammedanism avers that every pious good Mussulman, on being admitted into heaven, will be provided with nymphs or *houris*, according to his virtuous deeds ; but to him observing the fast an additional number will be allotted. The month of *Ramazan* has a celebrated* night termed "*shab-i-kadar*" or the night of greatness and pre-eminence, happening once only within the month. Opinions vary and traditions differ as to the actual night in question, but from reliable authorities it is asserted that *it* occurs on one day of the month, twenty-seventh being the surest day of its † occurrence. Influenced by the motive to benefit by the blessings of the happiest hour, all orthodox Mussulmans keep up for nights together watching for it, but the majority do not succeed, as the knowledge of the hour is confined to a select few. *Ramazan*, in a clearer sense, means the time only for worship and prayers and not for any earthly object. In *Ramazan*, Mussulmans must, so says their religion, thoroughly abstain, or try to abstain from wordly things and pursuits, as much as they can, in order that they may not be tempted to render unholy these fasts. Any person, who, notwithstanding all temptations, observes the *Ramazan* in its entirety, is said to be more meritorious than those who have fasted in retirement. In *Ramazan* every Mussulman is expected to strictly adhere to all the prescribed forms of prayers, to drain their coffers for the poor, and to do every sort of good he can to obtain his salvation in the world to come, and to enjoy God's favour in the world here. The only noticeable prayer of *Ramazan* which is a special service kept apart from others and exclusively held in connection with

---

* See *Alcoran*, Chapter 97.

† See Chapter "*Shub-i-Barat*," page 19-20, line 32.

the fasting, is what is called *tarawih*. This prayer or *nemaz* is kept with great ceremonial and pomp in all the Moslem mosques which are specially decorated: and on this occasion *hafizes*, (those who have got the Koran by heart) daily lead people in prayer and orally recite passages of the scripture. Prayers are held only in the night time when Mussulmans in a body repair to their respective mosques to hear the words of the Koran which they read or hear throughout the month. The first of *Shuwal* is the "*Eed*" festival, which is the day of pleasure and rest after the hard fatigue and sufferings of the *Ramazan*. On this day all Mussulmans, however divided they may be, are supposed to mix with and embrace each other. If one wishes to ascertain the true essence of Islam, he may call on this day at any Mussulman's house, where he may learn what Islam is, and how it is maintained and solemnised by its believers. This *Eed* day and the succeeding two days, are celebrated with great *eclat*.

As per usages and rules in force and use of all Muslim families, prayers of a special order and of an identical nature are held on the *Eed* and the *Bakur-id*[*] days; and the same are finished before 10 A. M., of these days. In some places and mosques these prayers are said early in the morning before sunrise; and in others *at different* hours, varying from 6 to 10 A. M. No prayers are, however, allowable after 10 o'clock, or at noon, from which moment commences the usual daily proper, the *zohur*, which nullifies any prayer other than itself. It is on this sole account that Mussulmans finish these two festival days' prayers before 10 o'clock as a matter of convenience and course. Let us here add that the annual celebrations *Mohurrum*,† *Ramadan, Eed* or *Idulfitır, Hujj* ‡, and *Bakur-id* or *Eeduzzoha*, are the only feasts which are equally and universally kept up by the entire body of the Muslim community; while there are many festivals which, if observed by one faction of the Mohammedans, are rejected by the other.

THE HUJJ.*

· Like the Ramadan,† this pilgrimage is one of the essentials of the Moslem faith, and is only obligatory for those having wealth and sufficient means of undertaking the holy mission. Well-to-do persons must *needs* visit the sacred place, Mecca, once at least in their life ; for so says Alcoran, and such are indisputably the holy Prophet's traditions. One dying without performing the pilgrimage, or *Hujj*, and having no valid cause for such failure, may as well die‡ a Jew or a Christian ! In Islamitic faith what God has specially ordained as a bounden duty of mankind for action in the universe is termed *furz*, meaning, thereby, an act to which every believer in Islam is impera- tively required to adhere firmly without failure, and the wilful renun- ciation of which renders the violator absolutely blameworthy and punishable ¶ by God. *Hujj* is likewise one of these *furzes* which

---

* (Vide the *Indian Daily News*, Tuesday, November 18, 1890, containing a paper on it by the Author)

† For the *Ramazan* see page 25

‡ See *Koran*, Chapter 2.

¶ Though every Muslim is bound to make the *Hujj* once during his life- time, still there is a saving clause—provided "able" so to do. The discussions as to the definition of the elastic qualification attached to the injunction of the Prophet have been endless and undecided. As a general rule, however, intending votaries must comply with four conditions: (1) Profession of the faith of Islam; (2) adolescence, generally fixed at the age of fifteen; (3) freedom from slavery; (4) mental sanity. To these some authorities add four more requirements, viz · (1) sufficiency of provision; (2) the possession of a beast of burden, if living more than two days' journey from Mecca; (3) security on the road; and (4) ability to walk two stages if the pilgrims have no beast. Others, again, include all conditions under only two particular heads: (1) health, and (2) ability. It is even maintained by some, that those who have money enough, if they cannot go themselves, may hire some one to perform the *Hujj* in their stead. But this privilege in the early days of Islam was very sparingly, if ever, used, and even now it is mostly considered amongst the orthodox sects that pilgrimage (*Hujj*) cannot be performed by proxy. None the less, however, if a Muslim on his death-bed bequeaths a sum of money to be paid to some person to perform the *Hujj* on behalf of his patron, it is considered to satisfy in a way the claims of the Muslim law. It is also decreed a meritorious act to pay the expences of those who cannot afford to obey the injunction of the Prophet.

all Mussulmans must maintain to the moment of their last breath. Such a *Huy* is provided by the religious law to be observed, made, and executed by money honestly earned or gained. Any fortune or valuables which may turn out to be bad and objectionable in the religious sense, if spent or given in God's way and in His name, only pollute, corrupt, and frustrate the eagerly coveted object of the donors. The givers lose in despondence the goal of their ambition which so prompted them to such an outlay in the idea of acquiring a heavenly reward in the world to come. Similarly, even alms-giving, involving debt or borrowing money from others, if such liabilities empty one's purse, and reduce him to an abject poverty, is entirely forbidden by the Islamitic ecclesiastical law. Thus strictly enjoins all to spend and give away from their stock in proportionate measure. *Apropos* of economy, the everlasting good outcome of all earthly pleasures, Islamitic principle is lucidly as follows :—" Reap freely the harvest of the field of your luck and enjoy out of it smoothly, and let others also partake of your merriment out of the treasure and wealth Providence has given unto and bestowed on you. But do on no account run so far beyond the limit of plausible moderation that you should ruin yourself and thereby become despicable, both to the Giver of all and to His creation ; and possibly become on that account so useless as not to be of service to your own self and to others."

The performance of this sacred duty of the pilgrimage devolves upon women* inasmuch as it does with men ; and this solemnity is, as a matter of rule, observed annually at Mecca in the 12th or last month of the year. It is brought to a final close on the 10th of the month termed "Zilhij," which month, as its very name imports, is peculiarly set apart for celebration of the ritual. Immediately on arrival at Mecca,

---

* A portion of the holy *Caaba* called ' Hashwatul-Haram," or "the women's sanded place,' is exclusively set apart for and appropriated to female devotees. But the weaker sex are forbidden to go alone , if, therefore, a woman has no husband or near relation to protect her, she must select some virtuous person worthy of confidence to accompany her, his expences being charged to her account.

the pilgrims visit the holy* Caaba round which they go in procession
seven times ; and take a like turn between the mounts Safa and
Marwa ; and halt at Mount Arafat where they slay the victims (of
the sacrifice), and shave their heads in the valley of Mina ; but before
entering Mecca, and on their near approach to it, they put on the
ehram, or sacred habit, which consists of two wrappers—one about
their middle and the other thrown over their shoulders, leaving their
heads bare. They wear slippers for covering and protecting their
feet against the toilsome dry sand. In the course of the use of
this sacred apparel, exclusively appropriated and reserved for the
auspicious moment alone, they avoid hunting and shooting ; and
this precept they keep and observe so punctually and rigidly that they,
during the ceremony, do not kill even any vermin. But some nox-
ious animals, as kites, ravens, scorpions, mice, and pariah dogs, they
are allowed to destroy and kill for the safety and preservation of their
lives against certain impending unavoidable dangers which, if neglected,
might be attended by lamentable results. During the pilgrimage the
pilgrims become so purely religious in every respect that they constantly
and strictly guard their actions and words, and totally refrain from
all quarrelling, or ill-language, and all converse with women, and
indecent, obscene discourse. They chiefly give their intention and
mind to the good work they have undertaken, labouring, as they do,
under the impression that any shortcoming in the discharge of the
ceremonial will deprive them of all the fruit of their earnest toil, the
subject of their trip to the holy place.

After the zealous observance of the foregoing prescribed rites
which last till the 8th of the Zilhij month, the pilgrims, at matin
of the following day, proceed to Mount Arafat where they say their
devotions till sunset ; and thence they march to an oratory called
Mozdalifa, lying between Arafat and Mina, where they spend the

---

* (i.e.) The sacred and inviolable mosque, called "Baitullah or Musjidul-
haram," containing a square stone-building, the Caaba which is of quadrangu-
lar form. For the full particulars as to architecture of this edifice, we re-
commend to our readers the use of a map of Mecca which would, doubtless, give them a clear intelligible idea of the form, size, &c., of the holy build-
ing.

light in prayer and in reading and reciting the holy Koran. At a
certain raised monument, they throw seven stones at three marks or
pillars, erected in imitation, and representation of Abraham who, so
goes the story, when about to sacrifice* his beloved son Ishmael, was
according to tradition there disturbed in his devotions, and in a manner
tempted to disobedience by the wicked devil whom he then drove
away by pelting stones at him. This finishes the pilgrimage, which
finally closes on the 10th of *Zilhij* † when the pilgrims, having slain
their victims ‡ and shaved their heads and cut their nails, take leave of
the holy Mecca, and make way for Medina to visit there the holy
tomb or shrine of the Prophet. As to this visit traditions abound to
the effect that visitors to it will experience a peculier advantage
and prerogative on the day of the resurrection, to wit : they will
be entitled to and deserving of the mediation and intercession
which the Prophet is told to make and give effect to on the
day in question, when, but for his intervention and pleading, the
cause of sinners, all believers in God and his followers will be able to
obtain salvation for their past sins and vices perpetrated and committed in the world. This visit to the tomb is said to be equivalent
to visiting the Prophet in person. On approching the shrine, pilgrims
invoke the blessings of both the Prophet and God. They say their
prayers, repeating passages and chapters from Alcoran, in honor and
memory of the departed holy Prophet. This visit is optional, and not so
obligatory as the *Hujj* and the other positive material religious precepts.

---

* See page 36, line 31 of the next chapter the "*Bukar-i-id* or Moslem
Christmas."

† The Mohammedan year being lunar and the seasons being regulated
by the sun, the time of the "*Hujj*" varies every twelvemonth, and occurs
in spring, summer, autumn, or winter, as the case may be, the entire
change being completed during a cycle of thirty-two years.

When a *Hujj* falls on a Friday, it is called "*Hujj-i-Akbar*" (grand and
great), and it enables pilgrims to acquire virtues and good qualities more than
they could gain in ten *Hujjes*. Such a grand *Hujj* Mohammedans had on the
17th of July of the just past year 1891 which, but for this auspicious
event, is especially remarkable and noteworthy in the Islamitic circle.

† These victims must be either sheep, goats, kine, or camels; males, of eithe
of the two former kinds and females if of either of the latter, and of a fit age.

THE BAKUR-ID
OR
THE MOHAMMEDAN "CHRISTMAS."*

On the tenth day of every Mohammedan twelfth month called Zilhij, is celebrated with great *éclat*, an d with almost all the possible pomp and show, the Moslem anniversary, well-known as the Holy *Iduzzoha*, or *Bakur-id*, on which occasion Mohammedans of all ranks and denominations are to be seen from early dawn till midday engaged in special† prayers. Every Mussulman, however poor he may be, is expected on this holy festive day to appear to the world´in resplendent apparel, to perfume his person and garments, and to give alms to beggars. The bulk of the believers in the *Koran*—however defective they may be in other secular Islamitic matters and religious proclivities—must refrain on this sacred day from all earthly concerns, and keep the day, to the best of their means and ability, in entire consonance with the prescribed forms and dictates of their religion, as (so goes their Faith), any departure from what has been rigidly preordained and exclusively reserved for the day's celebration, incurs heavenly displeasure for the transgressor, and renders him detestable and liable to excommunication. Influenced by the pure motive of observing the ceremony in its entirety, Moslems make extensive preparations for the feast, and endeavour, by decorum and in manners and dress, to present to the eyes of the nation an agreeable and interesting scene. Prayers, which close by‡ midday, are followed by offerings to the Maker of All in the shape of sacrifices of animals, which ritual lasts three consecutive days. These sacrifices, which are binding only upon well-to-do persons, when made by Indian Mussulmans, consist of cows, goats, and sheep ; but, if offered by Arab Mohammedans, consist of a variety of—nay, of almost all—quadrupeds allowable in religion, principal among them being camels, deer, &c. The offerer, after having these slaughtered, largely distributes the meat amongst his relatives, friends, and neighbours ; and on these three days of merry-

---

* Vide the *Indian Daily News*, Monday, July 28, 1890, in which appears an excellent nice paper on it by the author.

† For these prayers see page 30, para 2, line 16.

‡ See *Ibd.*

makings, *i. e.*, so long as such sacrifice is allowed in religion, presents from one to another are exclusively of flesh. *Anent* this sacrifice, there is rife amongst all Moslems a belief, founded on a unanimous verdict of Moslem doctors, and established upon an indisputable authority, to the effect that the animals so butchered serve the Mohammedans on the day of judgment, when they ride on them in crossing a bridge or pathway, called *Pul-i-sarat*, and running between heaven and hell, through which every Mussulman will have to go before approaching God to account for his or her respective past wordly actions ; and which none but the pious alone can safely pass. Traditions abound as to the existence of this bridge, and the only admittedly sound undeniable conclusion, as deduced from them, is that once passing the bridge is the third test out of several other trials which Mussulmans have to experience prior to their reaching God to answer for their deeds in the world. The first trial is the death moment, when, under awful agonies and pangs, dying men, if true Moslems, have to stand firm to their faith amidst all temptations on the part of the devil, who, according to Islamitic belief, then appears and does his best to lead astray the dying individuals, reducing them to disavow Unitarianism, and the advent to this world of God's representative, the Holy Prophet Mohammed. The second trial being in the grave where (so goes tradition), while the dead are buried, two angels from heaven resort to them to inquire about their faith, *i. e.*, as to what religion they embrace. The answer, if given in conformity with the Islamitic doctrine, paves the way for their everlasting pleasures and for calm undisturbed rest in the tomb till Doomsday ; but the answer, if otherwise, subjects them to a variety of privations and sufferings up to the day in question. The bridge above referred to is, as per religious tenet, thinner than hair, having some millions of miles distance between heaven and hell, and is invisible to unhallowed beings, whose success in crossing *it* rests materially with the service and assistance of the animals so killed on these three sacred days. The so-called sacrifice, so says religion, dates from time immemorial, and takes its origin from the time of the Holy Prophet, Abraham, whom God first enjoined to kill in His way and name one the dearest to him of all earthly objects, meaning thereby the sacrifice of his own beloved son, Ishmael, whom, when he was about to kill, was desisted from so doing by the Almighty Creator, who asked him to replace the son by a goat, which he slaughtered there and then. This, Mohammedanism says, was with the object of testing Abraham's obedience to God, who, seeing the trial so fully realised, pronounced him to be a truly obedient slave and friend of His, and, to perpetuate whose sacrifice, declared the same lawful for all Mussulmans having means and might of keeping and cherishing it. The *Idussoha* is, in a plainer expression, the time of the visit to Mecca, which visit is termed *Hujj*, or pilgrimage, and which is annually done by millions of pilgrims who repair thereto and make that *Hujj* on the 9th of *Zikad*, *i. e.*, one day previous to this day of sacrifice, which this year (1891) and the last year (1890) fell respectively on the 29th and the 18th July. This *Hujj* is obligatory wholly for men of substance and means, and is one of the very virtuous actions of good Mussulmans. (See the preceding chapter). In fine, what Christmas is to Christians so this *Bakurid* is to Mohammedans ; and hence, in non-Islamitic circles, it generally goes by the name of " Moslem Christmas."

THE "URS." *

Urs is a thorough Arabic word, which, though having one etymological sequence of the same primitive stock and derivation, and being of similarly one orthography, or spelling, is pronounced and uttered in two distinct methods. Its one elocution is *Irs*, meaning honeymoon, or the wedlock tie of the bridegroom and the bride, or the dinner served relating to a matrimonial rite. The second pronunciation is *Urs*, which tends to signify and imply a synodical gathering of Muslims, kept up in memory and honor of some departed saints.

The synonymy of the *Irs* being *Arous*, and the pluralism of both the forms stands the only one *Arais*. Synthetical composition in an intelligent comprehensive and lucid sense, of the theme, as compared with, and judged from the existing practices of the many Indian Mussulmans of the day indicates a dinner party, or *Mujlis*, observed annually by them in expression of their unaffected pure love and regard for most of their sainted persons, including parents, teachers, and other kinsmen of reputation, or of some respectable standing in woldly social career. This *Mujlis*, or meeting, which is convened every year on the exact date of the death of such departed personages, is celebrated with great solemnity by Muslims to perpetuate the memorable antecedents, and worthy name of the eminent persons so deserving of the special memento. On this occasion, the observer of such ceremonial invites his acquaintances, kinsfolks, and other admirers of the worshipped individuals to dinners, *soirees*, picnics, and different entertainments. Dancing men and musicians, known as *Kowals*, whose profession is completely given to such ritualism, are commonly, and as a matter of rule, hired by all observers to recite, read, and sing elegies, lyrics, odes, ballads, or sonnets in commendation of the virtuous and noteworthy deeds they (the worshipped characters) did while alive in the world. They (the Kowals) also dilate on the personal beauties with which they were naturally gifted, and the extraordinary powers of which they were singularly possessed, and which they gave vent to as astounding miracles to men of their

---

* Vide the *Indian Daily News*, Monday, February 2, 1891, containing the author's lecture on the subject.

time ; and these Kowals *likewise* detail the excellence and superiority
they (the adored individuals) had in point of their respective merit,
worth, and status in the wordly circle, and, more particularly, the virtues constituting them as men detached and snatched away from the
ordinary wordly beings, and as the ones entitling them to the adoration
and reverence of the populace, and befitting them for the occasions of
convivalities. Moulvies or other scholars solemnising this sort of feast,
give *it* an uncommon name which, in their own phraseology, they style as
Mujlis-i-urs. Large charity and prayers with earnest devotion, in honor
and memory of such departed saints, and for the general good of their
migrated souls, are primarily the actions of the fervid votaries or zealots
of the ritual. On the day the ceremony is held, the house where the
same is to be performed, is beautifully decorated with all practicable
embellishments ; and in the evening—in many families in the dead
of night—the tomb or shrine of the personages worshipped is washed
by the observers who, after this is over, repeat in conjunction with
other Moslems some chapters of the *Koran,* and go in procession
round the grave several times. After wiping up the water encircling
the tomb, they cover the tombstone with a new sheet made especially
for the occasion. It is only once in the year, and that even on this
opportunity that a new *chadur,* or sheet, is changed and given by the
solemnisers who have made this " *Urs,*" as the single instance
of supplying the repository of their saints with a cloak, as affording
the protection of the depository. The charnel-house being then
locked after the completion of this change of mantle, the chantry is
soon enlivened with hundreds of souls who chant masses for the
saints, as well as for the donors of the endowed property containing
the sepulchre of the object of veneration. After the usual prayers
have been said sweetmeats are distributed to partakers in the ritual,
and the old worn-out *chadur* (sheet) taken away from the burial-place,
is kept by fervent zealots as holy remains, which in parcels are sent
round and given to all followers of the saints as rich and valuable
presents, which, in most emergent cases, serve them as amulets
or charms against impending evils, or as safe defensible proofs against
the haunting of harmful goblins or spirits.

These usages, which are mainly practised by Indian Mussulmans, and hardly observed in Arabia the mother and fountain-head of Islam, consist of the existence of the varieties of essential materials to enumerate which would need elaborate detail. It will on this account be enough to say that followers of specific cannonised men have such festivals in commemoration of the anniversaries of the saints of the school to which they respectively and individually belong, and whose memory, as firm adherents, they deem it their duty to annually cherish.

Mohammedans styling themselves *Kadris,** *Chishtees,** *Nukhsh-bundias,** *Saharwardias,** and others, professing to be disciples and followers of some particular saints or religious preceptors and leaders of their schools, alone keep this *Urs*, as indicative of their obedience and homage to such saints from whom they have received their religious instruction, for the sect they adhere to.

Following these aspirant Moslems, other believers in Islam, too, have such celebration in honor of any of their leaders from whom originates their knowledge of their respective persuasions in Islamaism. Others, also strict in their religious proclivities, have such ceremonial in memory of their parents, teachers, and other elders in the family, whose position in the tribe happens to be deserving of a synodic observance of the kind. But none of these anniversary celebrations do in any way receive sanction from the *Koran*, nor do the same appear anywhere as an authority in any of the ecclesiastical books of faith.

Doctors of Divinity pronounce these rituals as blasphemous deeds, and hold perpetrators of such actions as sinners. The decisive view of all doctors is to the effect that, in absence of an authority to uphold and maintain these usages, and the same being not done at all in the time of the Prophet and his four Caliphs and immediate followers, none of whom appear to have done these things themselves, or licensed their followers for their observances ; these practices, if continued as they are now, would seriously render the perpetrators to the depths and abysses of miseries, troubles, and difficulties in the world to come, when they would be severely taken to task, and severely

* For these sects of Moslems see the foot-notes and the line 18 of the page 17.

handled by the Maker of the Universe, who has totally enjoined all His creations to be away from the contact and touch of all such profane and sinful things. Other sound, credible tradition is that the Prophet will not extend his hands of blessings to those creating, and causing to create, any innovated practices in Islam of the kind under notice. It, therefore, behoves all true believers in Islam to avoid these unauthorised malpractices, whose repetition will only subject them to no advantage, earthly or heavenly, but will on the other hand, make them less able to bear the bad effects resulting therefrom.

THE CHEHLUM.*

The *chehlum*—a Persian word which literally means fortieth—is the funeral obsequy observed by Moslems on the fortieth day, calculating from the date of an obitury of some of their kinsmen, friends, and acquaintances, and kept with great solemnity and *eclat* in honor and memory of such departed souls. It is a general belief amongst the community of Mussulmans, that, when a Moslem gives up the ghost, his soul haunts and lurks about the place where he breathed his last for fully forty days from the date of his demise : that it (the soul) comes to visit the quarter it left, with the idea and conviction that its surviving relations and acquaintances may show pity to *it* by offering prayers and charity for its good and salvation in the migrated region of the heaven above : that in case *it* finds *its* survivors doing good for its well-being, rest, happiness, and welfare in its changed career, *it* devoutly and heartily prays in return for their safety, pleasure, and comfort on the earth : and that, in the reverse case, when *it* perceives its people doing naught for it, or entrapped in vices opposed to the dictates of Islamitic faith, it curses them and invokes on them heavenly displeasure for their negligence and foolish reckless pursuits devoid of all religious principles. Actuated by this motive, Moslems—mostly of the rigid orthodox view and proclivity—devote themselves to doing some good, in the shape of prayers and charities, to their deceased relatives and friends ; and consequently, from the time and hour one dies or goes to the way of all departed, Moslems hire *Hafizes* (those that have got the *Koran* by heart), and *Moulvies* or *Mullahs* (learned priests) to offer the requisite prayers to the departed souls which are thus remembered for forty days, reckoning, as above said, from the actual day of the mournful event, requiring the celebration of such ritualism.

Before enlarging upon the performance of the *chehlum*, it would be much to the purpose and appropriate for the proper enlargement and narration of the theme itself, if contemporaneous and equal matters and rites of note and consequence, done and kept up in

* (See the *Indian Daily News*, Thursday, February 19, 1891, having a paper on the subject by the pamphleteer.)

connection with the *chehlum* under notice, be likewise detailed, either in their entirety, or sketched in brief, to give some idea of the sister celebrations solemnised *apropos* of the *chehlum* under remark.

Immediately a death takes place, people muster around to pay to the dead their last tribute, which consists of (a) saying a special prayer termed *nemaz-i-janazah:* and (b) of burying the coffin. On the burial day it is customary for relatives only to give moneys and clothes in charity for the good of the dead, and this they do before or after depositing their dead in the grave. Friends, whose connection with the dead was merely by acquaintance and not by blood, or family tie, also give away charities ; but such friends are generally rare. *Insan,* which means mankind, is made of "ins or uns," signifying affection : and the entire world coming under the category are supposed to be persons having and possessing some affection. Hence it follows, and is commonly held that Moslems in particular and the world in general, possessed as they are of affection so planted in them by Nature, should at least do something good to their brethren in any way they can ; and should nowise forget their forlorn departed friends or relatives in times of such difficulties, privations, miseries, and sufferings. Pious Mussulmans observe this with such strictness and devoutness that they ever make it their rule and sacred duty of being of some service or help to any one of any creed or color. It is only the self-aspirant men dying after earthly glories, and for selfish sordid interests and motives, that they stand neutral to good to none but to themselves.

From the day of death, *Hafizes* and *Moulvies,* who are hired on some fixed remuneration, begin reading the *Koran* till the *chehlum* or fortieth date ; and on the third or fourth day after the obitury is solemnised, a pleasing little rite called *chaharum,** on which opportunity Moslems gather round to recite and read passages and chapters of the *Koran* to the memory of the departed ; which being done, people separate with offers of betels and particular sweetmeats known as *nakooldanas,* which alone have now become the fashion with the Muslims to give away as presents to guests invited on the occasion.

---

* *Chaharum* means 'fourth.'

On the tenth day is performed the rite called *dasman*, when beggars are served with meals. Similarly, an occasion is observed on the twentieth or *bisman* day after the obitury ; and the last ceremonial is the *chehlum* when, like *bisman* and *dusman*, paupers are sumptuously fed and clothed ; and that brings to a close the ritualism in connection with dead persons.

Regarding such rites the verdict of the entire doctors of faith, as coupled with that of the leaders of Islam, is that these are thoroughly unlicensed and unlawful in the sense of the doctrinal faith ; and that, absolutely innovated as they are, they are completely abominable ; and the perpetrators thereof stand greatly punishable by the Maker of All.

What Islam allows in this connection is openly to the effect that (*a*) prayers and charities in memory of deceased persons may alone stand as good and performable ; (*b*) that for keeping even these under clause (*a*), it is needless to fix a certain period or time ; and that (*c*), the same can safely be done any time the doers like, and find themselves able to do to the best of their means and position.

Anent the haunt of the soul or *rooh* as above represented, opinions of doctors of divinity differ. Some hold it sound, and others pronounce the same as a thoroughly stupid idea, as they avow that, on the demise of a person, his soul or *rooh* is taken by death-angels to the *region* above, and kept closely confined there in a place called *Illin* * or *Sijjin*, from which the same is to be let off only on the judgment-day, when people will be summoned individually before the All-Powerful God to account for their deeds done in the phases, or runs of their wordly career. It is, so say doctors, only on this event that the *rooh* so confined is let off to return to the departed and left bodies to enliven and reanimate men to so answer for their earthly actions.

It now remains to be told, and properly expounded to the public as to the class of persons celebrating these negative disallowed usages.

---

* *Illin* means an abode in the sky for confinement of souls of good pious persons, when they die away from the world ; and *sijjin* is likewise another dwelling for sinners and unholy men.

It is none but the illiterate benighted portion of the Muslim Flock who, owing to their sheer ignorance of all Islamitic matters, so blindfully and superstitiously give themselves up to such observances. It is high time for the rising Indian Mussulmans, who alone have such celebrations which are foreign and highly unknown to Arabia, the mother and fountain-head of Islam, to stir up and do once for all these ceremonies opposed to the very text and spirit of the ecclesiastical law of faith.

THE "NEAZ."*

Neaz, which in Persian literally means supplication or humble request, practically particularises a current usage amongst Indian Mussulmans who observe it in prescribed forms, in memory of, and for salvation and good of departed saints, friends and relatives. The Moslems offer prayers, styling the same as *neaz*, which they say over sweetmeats and other eatables, &c., while in the act of holding *neaz*, at the end of which they distribute to others and enjoy themselves the eatables so consecrated by *neaz*. Most Moslems do not allow any portion of the *neaz* eatables to be given to strangers and to those not allied to them by relationship. Others strictly confine the *neaz* articles to pious Mussulmans, whether affianced or otherwise, while others again extend the same openly and liberally to all of any sect belonging to the Islamitic flock. The *neaz* is much more a vow than anything else, and it is the votaries who observe it in fulfilment of some pledge or promise made by them for the attainment of certain objects or purposes. Sometimes barren persons make vows for fecundity, and vows are formed for some earthly and private matters which, being obtained, the votaries hold the *neaz* in honor of the departed saints or the persons by invoking whose departed souls and through whose blessings and intervention they have been able to gain the coveted object. The performance of the *neaz* requires great and peculiar preparations. The votaries make arrangements for the occasion when oftentimes—though not invariably—they have play actings, merry-makings, dancings and shows, &c. *Neaz* said or done in case of deceased relatives and friends is entirely for the purposes of the deceased's salvation and good in their migrated career ; and is for no selfish interest or motive, as in the case of saints. The practice is so popular with Indian Mussulmans that, in all times of distresses and worldly troubles and anxieties, they keep the *neaz* as a prevention and safeguard against all difficulties disturbing them in the course of life. But such a ceremonious rite, that is barely in use in foreign and civilised climes other than India, is not conformable

---

* This appeared in the form of an article by the author in the *Indian Daily News*, Saturday, June 6, 1891.

with the Mohammedan ecclesiastical Law of Faith, so far as its modes of observance are concerned. The above specified ceremonial forms, and not the *neaz* itself, are objectionable in the sense and meaning of Islamitic doctrine. The approved manner of celebrating the *neaz* is that (*a*) sweetmeats and other eatables, &c., may not be used while holding prayers, which should be done by themselves without any addition in any way ; (*b*) that, after saying the prayers, whatever they might be, charities in food, clothes, money, &c., should be given to the needy and to those whose indigent circumstances deserve pecuniary aid ; (*c*) that the basis of the *neaz* needs essentially and always to be on the only true principle of doing good to departed souls, for whom the same is kept up, and nothing further ; and (*d*) that the *neaz* should nowise be confronted, intermixed, and confused with matters evidently against the spirit of Islam.

In having the *neaz* to the forms innate in them, Moslems of the day have become much more sinners than devout good celebrants.

Shirk, in Islam, means mixing other persons equally with God in His qualities and actions, and thinking others to be partly or wholly possessed of the powers exceptionally with Him and absolutely beyond human skill, means, control, ability, energy, and authority. Invoking the souls of sainted persons and others for succour in earthly matters or anything, and asking assistance in any form and shape from any except God, amount to turning aside from the Creator and to making others equal to Him, and thereby to be perpetrators of the *shirk*, the worst class of unpardonable sin, which, on no account, lets the doers enter Heaven, or rather subjects them to continuous sufferings, miseries and troubles in dungeon-hell. The *neazists*, by resorting to others for help, render themselves *shirkists*, and consequently become liable for the Providential punishment codified and provided for the *shirk* offence or sin. Common sense will never authorise and sanction the solicitation of help from inanimate objects like the worshipped saints or other persons. One personally helpless and entirely depending upon God, the Helper of All, can in no case be supposed to be of any service or use to those seeking his support. It is purely superstitious and foolish to hold otherwise. God, with

His extended hands of mercy and grace will, after due terms of punishment, forgive, so says religion, all sins other than *shirks* to which, as He expressly says in His Holy Book, perpetrators shall severely and for once be taken to task, and shall totally be deprived of His grace, favours and blessings in the world to come.

His glorified words touching the *shirk* are the following :—

" Knowest thou, oh ye ! children of the world : never prostrate for prayers to others except thy Maker, and of Him alone ask anything thou stands in need of. Do not thou compare any one with Him : consider and believe Him All-Powerful, and Highest of all the world contains. Respect Him as the doer of all, as the only one all in all ; shouldst thou pray to others and ask them for help, make thou then thy own separate gods, and flee from thy Maker, Who shall never look with favour upon thee in the forthcoming world. Beware of His wrath and the punishment He shall mete out to thee when thou appeareth before Him to account for thy worldly actions. Do never thou imitate idolaters who have blindfully left their Maker, and made myriads of gods for themselves. Thy Maker is ready at all hours to pardon thee when thou askest pardon of Him : and hence, unite thee in prayers to Him, and ask pardon of Him : for He is ever inclined to forgive."

In face of such an authoritative command, it is idle to imagine that the forms of the *neas*—and not the *neas* itself—are not objectionable,—nay, the same stand much more abominable, and should in right earnest be done once for all ; and the pure authorised modes like those above referred to be substituted therefore for the purposes that goad on and guide all celebrants of the ritualism.

THE " KOONDA."*

Koonda, as its name shows, means an earthen pot of a special form and *tout-a-fait* different from the mould and nature of other Indian vessels. It being a complete *Urdoo* or *Hindoostani* word, its origin is confined to India, the emporium of objects used in common life ; and *it* may not be mistaken for its brother phonetic word *koonda* which, though spelled alike in English, has a separate *Hindoostani* spelling with *th* or *d* added to it to transform its pronunciation and means a bulky piece of wood, used in Indian families for culinary purposes. Another identical word *Koonrra*, which means refuse, such as husks, hedges, &c., may not be misconstrued for *koonda* under notice. The *koonda* is a Mohammedan usage common to all Moslems inhabiting India alone, and is seldom met with among Mussulmans of foreign parts ; and the fact that it owes its existence to India, tallies with the reasoning that the usage is modern and chiefly Indian. This modern practice, which Moslems consider a part of their religion, consists of a peculiar prayer termed *Fateha* or *Neaz*, which they offer at any time and on any day of the year in honor of the holy fourth Calif Huzrut Ali, son-in-law and cousin of the Prophet. In this ritual Mohammedans congregate to read and recite passages and chapters of *Alkoran* in the name and in respect of the Calif, and after they have made the customary prayer termed the *Fateha*, they sit round to partake of the food or sweetmeats (as the case may be) prepared for the occasion, which sometimes consist of *pilao*, the well-known Moslem richly seasoned costly dish : and at others, of *phirni*, another exquisite dish dressed and cooked with milk, cream, &c., but the use of sweetmeats is general in the celebration of this singular rite. The food, sweemeats, &c., so prepared are placed in a large pot, the *koonda*, out of which all who partake of the ceremony are required to take their respective quotas, which they eat from one and the same place and plate together with all those present, and they are in no way authorised to take any such food or sweetmeats away to their homes or out of the room or place where the *koonda* rite is kept. There they are

---

* This appeared as an article by the author in the *Indian Daily News*, Tuesday, June 2, 1891.

sumptuously fed and fitly served, and that closes the celebration which, amongst all these, has for itself houses properly decorated, furnished, scented, and illuminated. Most Moslems extend this rite a little further and observe it too for Huzrut Abbas, a descendant of Huzrut Ali ; and do it commonly on the ninth day of the *Mohurrum*, but finish it actually on the fourth day after the *Mohurrum* celebration, *i.e.*, they commence on the ninth of *Mohurrum* when they close the *koonda* with the usual receptacle which they open, and make use of in the forms above adverted to, four days after the *Mohurrum* ; but a *koonda* for Huzrut Abbas, with such ceremonial, is very rare. As already said, the *koonda* is solely reserved for the last and fourth Calif, Huzrut Ali, and is performed only in the manner above narrated.

What adds to the general rejoicings of the commonality of Mussulmans and all civilised peoples, is that the differences and dissensions, as in existence appertaining to many religious matters, amidst the two rival factions—the Sunnis and the Shiahs—are entirely done away with on the occasion of the *koonda* ritual, which both sects conjointly and harmoniously solemnise without any hitch in their fraternity, and this, including a few other rites, is the only opportunity when both these sects unite agreeably.

As to the reality of the *koonda* usage, it may fairly be stated that the same, utterly innovated as it is, is anything but lawful according to the true spirit and essence of the Moslem ecclesiastical law of faith ; but saying or offering prayers in memory of a departed person, saint or otherwise, is nowise prohibited in religion, provided that such prayers be simple, solemn, unceremonial, and licensed to the extent of the standard rules and by-laws of the Islamitic faith.

THE *KOOL.* *

Kool, in Arabic and in the grammatical sense of the language, means "Say Ye!"; and customarily signifies a usage the Indian Mussulmans perform in connection with the funeral obsequies when deprived of relatives and friends &c. The *Kool* is like the *Neaz* noticed in the previous chapter; † and on this occasion, too, similar to the *Neaz,* they hold prayers in memory of the departed, to whom they do homage and pay respects by reciting passages and chapters entitled the *Kool.* In celebrating this ritual they have the same ceremonies as those observed on the fourth day of the *chehlum* rite previously ‡ noticed. The specific term of *kool* given to this ceremonial, is due because four principal chapters, beginning with the word *Kool,* are recited on this opportunity along with other parts of the *Koran.* These four *Kool* chapters, when literally translated, are respectively in the following words :—

I.

"Say, O unbelievers, I will not worship that which ye worship; nor will ye worship that which I worship. Neither do I worship that which ye worship. Neither do ye worship that which I worship. Ye have your religion, and I my religion."

II.

"Say, *God* is one God ; the eternal God. He begets not, neither is He begotten and there is not any one like Him."

III.

"Say, I fly for refuge unto the Lord of the day break, *that He may deliver me* from the mischief of *those things* which He has created ; and from the mischief of the night, when it comes on ; and from the mischief of *woman* blowing on knots ; and from the mischief of the envious, when He envies."

IV.

"Say, I fly for refuge to the Lord of men, the King of men, the God of men, *that He may deliver me* from the mischief of the whisperer who slily withdraws, who whispers evil suggestions into the breasts of men ; from geni and men."

---

* Vide the *Indian Daily News,* Thursday, June 11, 1891, containing the author's paper on the subject.
† See page 46.
‡ See page 42.

These above four quoted chapters are held in special veneration by the bulk of Mohammedans who use them in all prayers and regard them as the best portions of the *Koran*, but in admitting this to be correct to a certain extent, good orthodox Mussulmans,—especially those having a thorough knowledge of the Mohammedan Ecclesiastical Law of Faith,—believe that every part, word, line, passage, chapter and all that the Koran contains, are unquestionably correct in all respects ; and that, to misinterpret or to interpolate disbelieve or falsify in any way even an atom of the *Koran*, is a heinous, unpardonable sin which wholly vitiates such culprit's faith and gloomily situates him in the category of blasphemy which, on being established against any, renders such blasphemer worthy of and a permanent dweller, of the dungeon-hell in the life to come.

The *Koran*, the fountain-head and the very birth and root of Islam, is, so Moslems firmly believe, the exact and true word of God ; and reading it is just as speaking directly to God, and to obey it and believe in all what it contains is to believe in God and in the Prophet, His messenger through whom it (the Koran) is revealed to mankind. Hence it follows and is reduced on an admitted basis of facts and reasonings, that Moslems *must nowise* lessen the honour, dignity, and degree of any part of the *Koran* by giving it undue preference to other portions, all of which must needs be considered as equal and true in all points. Reading the *Koran* or reciting a part or chapter of it in memory of a deceased person, is nowhere disallowed in Islam, but is rather allowed and sanctioned by the holy prophet. What is only objectionable and unlawful, is the innovated ceremony or usage usually kept by Moslems in relation to such *Koran* reading. There is no use, as Moslems do at present, of having in connection therewith such informalities as for instance of keeping a dinner or picnic party or entertainment, and of inviting and convening other assemblies or *mujlises* (meetings) entirely opposed to the very dictates and provisions of the Mohammedan law of faith, which nowhere authorises the maintenance of a formality or an invented usage or custom that is rigidly required by Islam to be done *in toto*. Islam and its principles and requirements are so pure and simple, that even an idiot can comply with them with the greatest ease : and that, from Kings downwards, none can in any way grudge against the performance of the prescribed rules and regulations and bye-laws which usually govern all, are within the reach of every one. In dealing with Islam, it would be meet here to give in a few words the main doctrines and precepts relating to Moslem faith and religious duties essentially incumbent on all followers of the prophet.

To his religion the Prophet gave the name of Islam, which word signifies resignation, or submission to the service and commands of God. Islam the Moslems divide into two distinct parts ; *iman, i. e.*, faith or theory, and *din, i. e.*, religion or practice, and aver that it is built on fundamental points one belonging to faith, and the other four to practice.

The first is the confession of faith ; that "there is no God but the true God'; and that Mohammed is His apostle"; and to this Moslems add six different elements, *viz.*:—(1) Belief in God ; (2) in His angels ; (3) in His Koran ; (4) in His Prophet the Mohammad ; (5) in the resurrection and day of judgment ; and, (6) in His absolute decree and predetermination both of good and evil.

The four points relating to practice are : (1) Prayers which are said five times daily, *i. e.*, in the morning, at noon, in the afternoon, at eve, and in the night, to these prayers are added those washings or purifications termed *wazus* which are necessary preparations required before prayers ; (2) alms, consisting of cattle, *i. e.*, of camels, kine, and sheep ; of money ; of corn ; of fruits, *viz.*, dates and raisins ; and of wares sold, bargained, and bartered ; (8) fasting or *Ramadan* ; and (4) the pilgrimage to Mecca.

Before bringing the subject to a close, some thing should be added to the " *Belief in God*," the fundamental position on which is mainly erected the superstructure of the Islamitic religion which distinctly teaches that from the beginning to the end of the world, there has been, and for ever shall be, but one true orthodox belief ; consisting, as to matter of faith, in acknowledging the only one true God, and believing in and obeying such messengers or prophets as He should from time to time send, with proper credentials and laws, to reveal His will and commands to mankind ; and as to matter of practice, in the observance of the immutable and eternal laws of right and wrong, together with such precepts and ceremonies as God should think fit to order for the time being, according to different dispensations in different ages of the world.

Under claim that this eternal religion was in his time utterly corrupted, and professed in its purity, by no enemy of men, Mohamnied revealed himself as the just true prophet sent by God to reform those abuses which had tremendously crept into it, and to reduce it to its primitive simplicity with the addition, however, of peculiar laws and ceremonies as required and sanctioned by Nature for the prophet's action in this connection. The whole substance of the prophet's doctrine is principally under this one article of faith that is, "there is but one God, and that he the prophet, is the apostle of God." According to Islam the prophet and the holy religion he gave to mankind remain unsuperceded unalterable inviolable and imperishable till Doomsday.

MINOR AND PRIVATE CEREMONIES.

Under this head, the author wishes to include in this portion of the book all the festivals coming under the above category ; and to succinctly give our readers a rough sketch and some idea of the several other minor celebrations current amongst many Indian Mussulmans. We call these 'minor' because they do not tally with those noticed in preceding chapters, and form in no way the subject of observance by the Moslems at large. For the sake of brevity and convenience, let us first arrange these festivities in a group and proper order of form ; and then proceed to dilate upon all of them individually and separately.

The properly grouped form, will, therefore, come under one classification as follows :—(1) " *Bera-i-Khaja-Khizir*"; (2) "*Bakra-i-Shaikh-Suddo*"; (3) "*Zearut-i-Kaboor* or *Mannit-Mangna*"; (4) "*Mela-i-Dargah* or *Mannit-Charhana*": (5) "*Hazerat-i-bhoot-o-jin*"; (6) '*Rujjabi*'; and (7) '*Nowroz*'.

BERA-I-KHAJAH-KHIZIR.

The above literally means a raft floated in honor of Khajah Khizir, one of the prominent Prophets of the Muslim bulwarks of faith ; and ordinarily signifies a peculiar rite current among Mussulmans of India. To understand the subject in its entirety, let us at the outset give our readers some idea of the antecedents and characteristics of Khajah Khizir, the hero and object of the ceremonial under notice. The Holy *Khizir* ranks amongst the many renowned Prophets of old, and is one of the recognised Apostles of God : but what will strike our readers as strange is that the Holy Khizir, who appeared in the universe as Deputy of God hundreds of years ago, is, so says Islam, still in existence and will live till the Judgment Day. To understand this, it should be borne in mind that, according to the faith of Islam, Alexander the Great, surnamed "*Zool-Karnain*"*,

---

* *Zool-Karnain*—Literally meaning, one possessed of two 'curls' because Alexander is said to have had such curls on his hair. Some say that he was 'two-horned,' and his head was figured as 'Ammon with the Ram's Horns on coins and medals.' Others trace the origin of the word to "*Karan*" meaning the two worlds, since he is said to have ruled over the entire world and is further stated to have measured both land and water. Hence, this surname which only finds its place in the *Koran* that calls him by this name particularly.

in Moslem phraseology, was a contemporary of the Holy Khizir who was on terms of intimacy with the Greatest of all the Monarchs that had then flourished on the surface of the earth. *Khizir* gave him an account of "*Ab-i-haiat*" or 'Water of Life' which, according to his statement, then existed in a certain part of the world; quite obscure and unknown to any: and which had the effect of rendering immortal those who drank of *it*. Consequently, both proceeded on their way in quest of the said holy water according to the direction and address *Khizir* knew and gave. It is said that both walked for some distance together: and while, midway to their destination, came across two paths running in a zigzag line. *Khizir*, the Guide, admonished Alexander his fellow-passenger to go over the line he pointed out; but Alexander, who was obstinate and pretended to know better than his Guide, did not heed his advice: and chose the course which to him seemed good in defiance of his Guide's direction and advice. The result that followed, as the outcome of the change in the courses the two had pursued, was that *Khazir* carried off the palm and successfully returned after drinking the Holy Water: while the unrelenting Alexander came back utterly disappointed and dejected. Another tradition is that both went to the Holy Water which *Khizir* drank at once, but the Mighty Alexander hesitated as the water appeared to him polluted and unclean. After *Khizir* had drunk some, he expostulated with the King to have a drink of it but at last! when, after great remonstrance and arguments on both sides, the King went to drink it, God infinitely resented and detested the King's vain glory and haughtiness, and caused the water at once to disappear from his vision. The sequence of the aforesaid conflicting traditions, is that the King was unluckily deprived* of a drink of

---

* The famous author *Al-hafiz*, who, is the shakespeare of Shiraz, commemorates the incident in the following lines in one of his poetical works.—
"Tahi dastan-i-kismut ra   chasood az rahbarai kamil;
Ke khizir az ab-i-hewan   tishna min arud sikunder ra."
(TRANSLATED)
'What use there is of a veteran guide for an unlucky person because *Khizir* has brought Alexander back from the "Water of Life" as thirsty as he went.'
This is equivalent to the Latin proverb: "Nisi domini frustra" *i. e.*, unless God be with you, all your toil is in vain.

the Water. Now, to turn to the main subject, the said *Khizir* is since then alive and will remain so till the end of the world. In accordance with Moslem traditions, the said *Khazir* has a brother named Khajah Illias of equal qualifications : and both the brothers have been entrusted with power to do good to the inhabitants of our globe. *Khizir* is in charge of Land, and Illias, of Water ; and both help suffering humanity out of their miseries and difficulties in land and water respectively. But here exists a great discrepancy. Some believe *Khizir* alone to be in absolute charge of Water and Land : and to others, Illias is assistant and partner of *Khizir* in all our worldly connections. In fine, *Khizir* and Illias make one individual person in charge of the globe, whatever may be his or their respective and individual merits, goodnesses and virtues &c. It is a belief current amongst Moslems that, in sea-voyages, *Khizir* protects ships from being wrecked ; and shields voyagers from being drowned or washed overboard. Travellers, in land, too, have their hardships guarded against by the *Khizir* who, in addition to the many offices Providence has placed in his hands, undertakes teaching all those whose destiny enables them to be taught by him in the arts, and sciences, &c., in which Nature has endowed him with knowledge superior to any human being. He is also said to have been tutors to many Prophets, Saints, &c., whomsoever God directed from time to time to be taught by him. Inspired by this idea, Moslems to this day live upon hopes of being so honored and graced by his teachings : to attain which they have a special prayer in honor of the *Khizir* whose help they invoke : and many-lucky persons have, so say the traditions, succeeded already in their prayers ; and others still expect to prosper, if they acted upon the prescribed instructions laid down in this connection. However that may be, we have nothing to say against these traditions. What our province is and which alone we are called upon to treat here, is the ceremony under notice, and nothing else. Influenced by a pure love of doing homage to their Sentinel and Lord of Waters, Indian Mohammedans prepare rafts or *Berus* which, laden with burning lamps and bouquet of flowers and full of fruits sweetmeats and other eatables, they float on rivers, rivulets, oceans, seas, &c., in memory of *Khizir* whose blessings they say they acquire by so doing. In thus cherishing the immortal name and memory of their everlasting *Khizir*, they keep up a festival on a grand scale which consists of general merry-makings accompanied by dinners and entertainments given to their relations and friends ; by charities, to indigent persons, and by musics and dances &c. Following the great procession, are people of different classes and age who, in a body, repair to the banks of rivers, or the seaside, with all sorts of nice presents, in money, clothes, and eatables &c., which, on arrival at their destination, they consign to the Water in hope of their being duly accepted and received by *Khizir*. While, on shore and before consigning their presents to the water, they recite prayers in honor of *Khizir* and beg his assistance in all worldly concerns. The position of the Mohammedans so doing, stands on a par with that of the Hindoos worshipping their Holy Mother Ganga. But this form of ritualism *does* in no way find favour with the belief of Islamism which is directly opposed to such a usage ; it is anything but lawful, and the doers thereof are classed as sinners before God. Prayer to any saint, holy Prophet, and pious personage, is nowise objectionable : but the ceremony referred to above, which has not received sanction from any leader or doctor of Islam nor is it compatible with the provisions of the Mohammedan Law of Faith, is thoroughly improper and wrong in every sense and letter of Mohammedanism ; and should, on this account, be interdicted by our community.

BAKRA-I-SHAIKH-SUDDO.

As in the account given elsewhere of * ' *Bera-Khajah-Khizir*,' we will begin this chapter by giving a sketch of *Shaikh Suddo* to whom this ritualism owes its origin ; and who is also the hero of this ceremonial.

Of the many selections made out of his biographies from various Hindustani works on the subject, it appears that the *Shaikh* figured in the olden times as an Arabic scholar ; and, by his mastery over *Koran* and other Holy Books, he was able to perfect himself in certain pas-

---

* See page 53.

sages which endowed him with superhuman power and miraculous skill.

Thus, for instance, there are in the Koran some verses by the help of which ghosts, genii, and all evils can easily be cowed down, exorcised, or brought under the yoke and subjugation of those reciting these passages : there are numerous others which could enable the latter *i. e.*, persons reciting to obtain whatever they want from a worldly point of view. Those who have acquired these virtues are termed " *Amils ;* "* and the office and dignity of such ' *Amils* ' depend upon the penance they have to undergo for years under difficulties and privations.

The qualifications of these holy men vary according to their different acquirements and merits. Some have the power of ruling over all genii, ghosts and spirits and of getting their purposes answered through their instrumentality. Shaikh Suddo falls under this denomination. There is a legend that this Shaikh fell in love with a young girl of unsurpassing beauty, the daughter of a king of his time. Of poor and humble parents, the Shaikh could never dream of marriage with her. Access and entrance to the royal *harem* or *zenana* or even to the courtyard of the king's palace buildings seemed almost impracticable for him : and, when he failed to gain his object by fair means, he resorted to his *Amilism* and sought the help of evil spirits. By their aid he had her brought to his cottage every night when she was fast asleep and sent her back to the palace at dawn. To her all this appeared as a dream. Being overvexed in mind, she reported the circumstance to her parents who caused the *Shaikh* to be apprehended and executed forthwith. The notorious *Shaikh*, it is said, was unclean and impure at the time of his sudden death, or, through the help of the genii, he might have escaped the capital punishment meteod out to him. To cut the matter short, the *Shaikh*, so ignorant Moslems believe, still haunts

---

* *Amil*—literally means a doer of a certain act ; and it signifies religious mendicant of the type referred to here.—In Indian Law, *Amils* mean Collectors or farmers of Government Revenue : and the word is derived from ' *Amal* or *Umal* ' which legally means ' management ; authority ; possession.' Such a class of revenue officers and functionaries existed mainly during the reign of the former Mohammedan rulers and Nobobs of Bengal.

and worries their women. He is also supposed to harm children. To dispel and drive him away from them, the Moslem worshippers of this devil have an annual ceremony in memory of him, which they term ' *Bakra-i-Shaikh Suddo*,' the subject of this chapter. On this occasion they slaughter kids and goats which, in Hindustani, are called ' *Bakras*.' A regular feast is kept up consisting of cooked food, breads, sweetmeats, &c. over which they say special prayers which, being over, they distribute the meal amongst idigent persons and partake of them themselves. It is sometimes accompanied by music and dancing, and by the recitals of poems composed in commendation of the virtues and excellences of *Shaikh*. Oftentimes women, 'possessed' by the Shaikh, are taken to the place of the performance which, they imagine, will instantaneously cure their sufferings. From a religious point of view it is totally unlawful to celebrate such an unlicensed custom that nowhere finds any support in the pure doctrines and principles of Islam. Those who perform this ceremony are, as a matter of course, classed with sinners and are in consequence liable to severe punishment by God. Enlightened Mohammedans do not believe in the existence of goblins, ghosts, &c. The ceremonial is purely an Indian affair and is not observed by any one out of this country, the mother of all superstitions and foolish ideas. Innovators of unauthorised practices are considered as '*Biddatis and Mushriks* ' or, in other words, they are great sinners and can not be admitted to Heaven. They are doomed to go to the infernal regions to suffer everlasting punishment there.

HAZERAUT-JIN-O-BHOOT.

Our next task is to notice this ritual which is analogous to the ceremony described above. It will, therefore, suffice to say that Moslems observing it try by the same means to exorcise ghosts and evil spirits ; this is done by saying prayers upon men, women, and children ; and here, too, they resort to *Amilism* and its practices as they do with the "*Bakra-i-Shaikh-Suddo*." Both of them are unauthorised and disallowed by the Mohammedan Faith.

NOWROZ.

The term *Nowroz* literally means ' *a new day*,' and indicates the anniversary held by Mohammedans in honor of the day of the installation to the Caliphate of Huzrut Ali,* the fourth and last successor, to, and son-in-law and cousin of the Prophet. According to the Muslim Calendar this auspicious event falls on some day in *Shaban*, the eighth Mohammedan month corresponding to English March or thereabouts. This festival is solemnised by *Shiahs*† in particular and by most of the *Sunnis* as well. Though *Shiahs* and *Sunnis*, the two principal sects of Mohammedanism, are divided in their creed, they still have equal regard and sympathy for Huzrut Ali. On the occasion referred to above, Muslims illuminate and decorate their houses ; and read passages from *Alkoran* and other religious books in praise of the Holy Calif and touching on his remarkable personalities, virtues and miraculous deeds which he revealed in his lifetime. Subsequent to those recitals, follows a peculiar prayer termed ' *fateha* ' which is said in honor of the Caliph's soul : and, after the close of the ceremony, sweetmeats are given away to the guests and others joining in it. Saying prayer to the departed soul of a saint, apostle, or even an ordinary person, is in no wise objectionable in Islam. Orthodoxy consists in one's performing what is required of him by the faith of Islam, and nothing more ; for the neglect of which, he will be severely dealt with by God.

Similarly is the anniversary *Rujjabi* which most Moslems hold on a certain day in *Rujjub*, the seventh month of the Mohammedan year corresponding with the month of February in the English calendar. This ceremonial, which is solemnised once a year about the time aforementioned in honor of the Holy Prophet's celebrated ' Miraj‡ Night,' is quite consistent with the custom prescribed for the *Nowroz ;* and it needs no further comment here.

---

* For a full account of Ali see, amongst numerous English books, Sale's *Koran*.

† For a detailed narrative of the differences subsisting between the *Shiahs* and *Sunnis* vide the foot-note to the Chapter entitled the *Mohurrum*, page 6.

‡ For *Meraj-Night* see *Milad*, page 141, line 24.

ZEARUT-I-KABOOR
OR
MANNIT-MAGNA.

Zearut means a visit, and *Kaboor*, tombs ; and *Mannit-Magna* signifies ' *asking help of :* ' and the whole expression, when combined, means ' to visit shrines of some saints and prophets and to beg assistance of them respecting concerns, worldly, personal or sacredotal.' It is a common belief of the benighted Mussulmans that holy persons, possessed as they are of supernatural powers, could help them, while they are alive and also after their death. They say that ' saints are immortal ', and that they do not die but are changed in the eyes of the world ; and that, like Prophets, saints are entrusted with responsible offices for the safety of the lives of mankind and for the management of the worldly affairs : that these saints serve God in various capacities suited to their respective individual abilities, qualifications and ranks : and that some are like sentinels, some, inspectors ; others, as superintendents ; and so forth. These beliefs are worth especial notice, which we transcribe from the original tenets of the *Koran* itself and of the dicta of the Mohammedan Laws of Faith. *The Koran* is very explicit in this respect. It clearly says " Everything is mortal and immortality belongs to God alone." ' Everything ' includes angels, prophets, saints, men, and whoever and whatsoever are born and created on the surface of the earth. Here the *Koran* makes no exception but gives a general commandment applicable to all of whatever denomination or cognomen. It is also evident that all Prophets, from Mohammed upwards and including himself, have already died like ordinary men ; and such has, too, been the fate of Mohammed's own caliphs, relations, successors and descendants.

If such an '*immortality*' is only confined to '*walis*' or saints, why was it not likewise extended to Prophets, the best of all human beings. No answer can be given to this. Mohammed, the father of Islam, died like an ordinary man ; and suffered pangs and sorrows more than all his followers, and taught his disciples never to think that he did not die or that he had transformed his soul into some other shape or form. His elegant words bearing on the point run thus :—

' Know ye ! all my believers that I die as my predecessors have died ;
and that all who have come to the world, must die one day : and that
merely God—and no body else—is everlasting.'

Then referring to his death throes and pangs which he suffered at
his last moments, his glowing words are :—' Oh Angel of Death, use
all violence and trouble you can to me on this day, but promise me *not
to* molest and cause pain to my adherents and followers at the point of
their death : I cheerfully and freely allow you, my good friend Angel,
to subject me this day to all sorts of miseries and affliction for the sake of
my poor children, the followers who are dearest to me of all'. To this the
angel replied :—' My King and Lord ! God is willing to let Your
Majesty, His intimate, best and dearest friend, remain in the world
permanently if you so like ; and I am commanded by Him to only
convey to you the message of His impatience and eagerness to see you :
should you resent and decline leaving the world, I would go back to
Him with this expression of yours, as I am strictly enjoined by Him
to observe all homage and respect due to your Majesty's supreme dignity.'
Here, interrupting the angel, the Holy Prophet adds :—' I am myself
most anxious to see my friend (God) so soon as practicable : so pray,
do your duty soon but adhere to the promise in reference to my followers.' To this the angel replies :—' Believe me, My Lord ! that I shall
take your followers' lives so lightly that they will feel nothing.' The
Prophet, infinitely pleased at this assurance, with an outburst of joy
here exclaims :—'And so do I happily suffer you to inflict all troubles
upon me to-day.'

Before reverting to the principal subject, let us note here that
what the Crucifixion of Christ was for the salvation of his followers'
souls, so was this in case of Moslems whose Most-Merciful—Benignant
Lord the Holy Prophet has so rigidly and bitterly suffered at his
death-bed for the exclusive sake of theirs.

The above adverted to belief as to immortality of saints or *walis*
has nothing to uphold it in face of such an express undeniable commandment ; and hence it is a pure fiction. Anent the Wali's offices
of trust as those above-mentioned, nothing of a reliable character is

found in Islam and may be disposed of as a pure fiction, as the following quotations from God's own Holy Commandments will show :—" Whatever I have predestined, must have its course without let or hindrance ; none but me (God) can do anything ; ask, therefore, of me all you want and I will give it to you : but if you go to a third person for assistance, make then your own separate God, and go direct to hell once far all." The Prophet's own example also fully illustrates this. He never said that he could do anything. He ever professed humility and simplicity, and openly avowed that he was a slave of God as every one was ; with this only one exception that he was His Viceroy or Prophet deputed by Him to show the world a good path and to stand a guarantee for their salvation in the next world. Though the Prophet performed thousands of miracles but he never said that he had done them himself. All that he declared was this :—" When people doubted my Apostleship Inspiration and Prophecy and demanded miracles of me, I applied to God and He, out of His own mercy, has shown them all that they wanted from me in truth and proof of my Prophecy and Viceroyality."

In fact, help in any way and matter emanates direct from God consistent with the supplicants' own share of what Nature has pre-ordained in their destiny which remains unalterable and which none save God can change for good or worse in the best way He chooses. Verily, Prophets' and Saints' prayers are readily listened to. But when ? Only in special cases and that even must wholly coincide with one's portion of the fate foreordained and prescribed by God under His immutable Decrees.

Ignorant Muslims in particular visit shrines of these Saints or *Walis*, and beg their assistance in personal matters ; and when their object is gained, they perform their vows by presenting to the shrine sweetmeats, *chadurs* (sheets of clothes) and other offerings they can according to their means. Music and dances also enliven this occasion. Assistance which they so demand of the Saints, is too often confined to success in some law-suits or other business matters or in cases of sickness, or when they have to contend with difficulties in their struggles for daily bread. Sometimes, women who are considered barren go to solicit the Saints to remove the curse from them and bless them with offsprings.

Under the above description comes the rite known as

MELA-I-DARGAH
OR
MANNIT-CHARHANA

which has the same significance as the ceremonial described in the preceding article ; with only this difference that *Mela-i-Dargah* implies ' a fair ' happening at some fixed time in the year in conjunction with a shrine or holy resting place of some Saints to preserve their memory by means of and resorting to and adopting the above noticed customs and usages :' and ' *Mannit-i-Charhana* ' conveys the meaning of a fulfilment of a vow made in respect to sanctified personages upon attainment of some specified object ; and which the parties making the vow perform according to methods as those mentioned above.

POSTSCRIPT.
Thanks to whom thanks are due.

___

THE NAWABS OF DACCA.

Of the Mohammedan notabilities of Bengal who take great interest in the author personally and in his present work in particular, are Their Highnesses Sir Nawab Abdool Ghani, Bahadoor, K. C. S. I., and the Hon'ble Nawab Ahsanulla, Khan Bahadoor, C. I. E., of Dacca ; both of whom have favoured the author with their* portraits for use in this pamphlet, and have further kindly subscribed a suitable amount of † money for meeting the costs of printing this little book. The author thanks them heartily for their generous gift, and fervently hopes they will condescend to continue their patronage towards the aspiring author.

___

AHSUN MANZIL,
DACCA,
MY DEAR SIR, 11th *February* 1891.

* I have received your letter of 4th instant and as requested I send you per book post two Photos, one of myself and the other of my father and hope they will reach you safely.

Yours truly,
To (Sd.) AHSANULLAH.
MOULVIE S. M. AMEER ALI, SAHEB,
Laharia Serai,
Durbhungah Courts.

___

AHSUN MUNZIL,
DACCA,
MY DEAR SIR, 5th *March* 1891.

† I have much pleasure to enclose herewith C. Notes for Rs. 30 (Thirty), on account of my donation towards the publication of your work "The Moslem Festivities." Please acknowledge receipt.

Yours truly,
To (Sd.) AHSANULLAH.
MOULVIE S. M. AMEER ALI SAHEB,
Laharia Serai,
Durbhungah.

To speak the truth, we Bengal Mussulmans have in both the father and the son distinguished patrons and true sincere friends who are always ready to help us in the best way they can. May the noble Nawabs live long to enjoy the success they deserve. Amen !

In noticing. the illustrious liberal Nawabs, the author of this pamphlet avails himself of a fit opportunity to thank, on his own behalf and on that of the whole Mohammedan community, our much esteemed and popular Viceroy Lord Lansdowne, for the judicious selection he has made in raising the Hon'ble Nawab Ahsanullah, Khan Bahadoor, c. i. e., to a seat in the Supreme Legislative Council, and for conferment upon both the noble Nawabs of the titles of "Nawab Bahadoors" in connection with the usual Honors of the New Year's Day of 1892. It is needless to say that they are the just recipients of the 'Honors' so bestowed on them, and to anticipate that, in view of their numerous deeds of charities already done and still being daily done, they, by degrees and hereafter, will soon have for them 'Honors upon Honors' at the generous hands of our Parental Charitable Government. It is again idle and useless to add here that, as Member of the Legislative Council, the Hon'ble Nawab Ahsanullah has already made a successful and valuable colleague of His Excellency the Viceroy.

THE HON'BLE NAWAB SYED AMEER HOSSAIN, KHAN BAHADUR, c. i. e.

Our esteemed valued friend, the worthy Syed Ameer Hossain, Khan Bahadur, the popular Presidency Magistrate of Calcutta and the energetic able Secretary, Central National Mohammedan Association, deserves our warmest thanks for the very many favours with which he has already obliged the author in various ways ; and, above all, for the keen interest he has always in view and at heart for the author personally and for this little book particularly. His large sympathies for the good of his co-religionists and the profoundest regard and estimation in which he is evenly and commonly held by all classes of people, are too well-known to need any comment. He has always our best wishes for his general prosperity in life.

MR. JAMES WILSON.

Of the numerous journalists of India who have kindly given in their valued journals notices of the publication of this pamphlet, the name of our esteemed and worthy friend, Mr. James Wilson, Editor of the "*Indian Daily News*," deserves mention ; since, by his wonted goodness and courtesy, he has laid the author under a deep debt of gratitude. The personal kindly regard he has evinced for the author and his co-religionists, may be gathered from the fact that he has freely opened his columns for the author's writings on Islam ; and, as our readers will observe from this pamphlet, all the subjects herein discussed are principally reproductions from his widely circulated journal in which he has kindly already published *in extenso* the groundwork of the present *brochure*.

In fine, what the popular Mr. Wilson has already done and is still doing for the author, can, in no case, be done by Moslems themselves whose religion it is now the writer's task to lay open to the general reading public. It goes without saying that in Mr. Wilson India has a valuable, sincere friend who, by his sympathy, has infinitely endeared himself to the whole nation.

THE LATE MR. ROBERT KNIGHT.

In this connection it would be ungracious to omit the name of another "Friend of India" the late lamented Robert Knight, Editor of the "*Statesman*." The author's acquaintance with him commenced in 1886 when he wrote a great deal on the then burning *Mohurrum* question, and lasted till his melancholy demise in the early part of 1890. The deceased gentleman was the first to notice in his journal the author's papers on the *Mohurrum* and the *Ramadan* which are herein included.

THE 'ENGLISHMAN.'

The learned Managing-Proprietor of the "*Englishman*," Mr. J. O'B. Saunders, and its able editor Mr. A. Macdonald, also deserve the pamphleteer's best thanks for the kind reference they have made in their highly respected journal of the author and of his this work. The author thanks them especially for their publication in the *Englishman* the author's three papers entitled the "*Mohammediss Ahι-ι-hadιs*" written by him sometime ago touching on the Islamtic faith and the different sects into which Moslems are divided.

OTHER FRIENDS.

Of his many European personal friends, to whom the author is already gre atly indebted in various ways, and who are the admirers and well-wishers of the author by their goodness and courtesies, may be mentioned the worthy names of (1) the Revd. J. Muir Hamilten, B. D., Natural Science Professor of the Calcutta General Assembly's Institution, now in Edinburgh ; (2) Signor Olinto Ghilardi, Assistant Principal, Government Arts School, Calcutta, (3) Mr. A. J. Leitgeb, Proprietor of the firm known as "*A. J. Leitgeb & Co.*," and the Calcutta Agent to several Italian Firms ; and (4) Mr. A. S. Stephen, late Assistant Editor, *Statesman;* and Special Calcutta Correspondent to the *Pioneer*, the *Morning Post*, the *Bombay Gazette* ; and now Editor of the *Liberal* and several Metropolitan weeklies.

BABOO NORENDRO NAUTH SEN.

The author's esteemed friend, Baboo Norendro Nath Sen, Attorney-at-law and Editor of the "*Indian Mirror*" also deserves the author's warmest thanks ; since, amongst native journalists, he was the first to favourably notice this little book. Good, amiable, and courteous, a perfect gentleman, that he is, the writer is already particularly indebted to him in various ways.

THE 'PAIK-BEHAR.'

The Proprietor-Editor of the Patna-Vernacular paper the "*Paik-Behar*," Moulvie Mohammed, a personal valued friend of the author, deserves special mention here. The author is under a deep lasting obligation to him for his many favours in various ways.

BABOO ISHAN CHUNDER MOKERJEE.

(A RETIRED OFFICER, ACCOUNTANT-GENERAL DEPARTMENT).

(Of 106-107, Mechua Bazar Road, Thunthania, Calcutta.)

It will be simply ungrateful on our part to totally omit here this venerable gentleman, a particular friend and great patron of the author whose general success and well-being in all departments shades and walks of life do invariably form his favourite subjects ; and, in the whole of the Calcutta City of which he is one amongst the distinguished notabilities, he is the only best support and help to the author in all his movements of life. May his shadow never grow less. Amen !

THE AUTHOR.

THE LATE MOULVIE DEEN MOHAMMED KHAN BAHADUR
(IN MEMORIUM.)

The deceased Moulvie's thinness and thickness with the author and the mutual highest affectionate regard with which we the two boon hearty companions passed under the same hearth and roof a long quiet happy life and were thus the means of sharing each other's pleasures in all wordly concerns, being already too well known to many, it would be futile to recapitulate here anything in reference to how we were uncommonly connected with each other till his last breath which, for the poor surviving authour, is a blow heavier than the loss of our own nearest and dearest relations. However as it is, we can not conclude this portion of our work without paying the unfeigned just tribute we dutifully owe him. Our means and province being very limited, we are unable to concert a suitable measure to perpetually cherish his worthy name ; and nor we feel ourselves called upon to encroach upon the indulgence of our readers with a lengthy memoir of his. Influenced by a sincere desire to do something to immortalise his respected memory, we only rest content with reproducing below what we, as contributor to the *Statesman*, supplied to the said journal regarding the deceased lamented Moulvie whose notice the able issue of the paper dated, Saturday, the 26th October 1889, contains as follows :—

"OBITUARY.—It was on the 1st instant we noticed the death of Ghulam Mohammed, the only son of Safiruddowlah Moulvie Din Mohammed Bahadoor, and now it is our painful duty to announce the death of the father. He never rallied from the shock at the loss of his son. His health declined fast and after a few days' fever he died on Thursday last at his residence at Komedan Bagan Lane. The deceased entered the local Madrassa College while yet a child, and after a few years' scholastic career he rose to be assistant principal of this institution, then under the charge of the late General W. Nassau Lees, L. L.D., with whom he was a great favourite, and it was only a couple years ago that the General sent to the Moulvie Saheb an engraving taken from his photograph, in the full dress of an officer of the Bengal Light Cavalry, with the following words inscribed underneath. "Your affectionate uncle W. N. Lees." The late Moulvie was one of the first natives of Bengal who was appointed a deputy magistrate during the Lieutenant-Governorship of Sir Frederick Halliday. His next appointment was Sworn Examiner of Privy Council translators in the High Court. He then became Private Secretary to the late King of Oudh on the recommendation of Sir Ashley Eden, who pronounced him "very smart, most respectable and the most trustworthy of all the King's servants." The deceased Moulvie also acted as Secretary to the Commission appointed by the Government of India for the settlement of the debts of the late Nawab Nazim of Bengal. He did yeoman service in this capacity and effected a saving to Government of several lakhs of rupees. His remains were interred yesterday at 1 P. M., at the family burial ground at Khirkee Talab in the suburbs, the *elite* of the Mohammedan Society, representing the Oudh and Mysore families and others, besides a concourse of between two and three thousand persons of all grades and life, attended his funeral. The deceased was the senior member of the Central National Mohammedan Association. He had just passed his sixtieth year. In him the Mohammedan community has lost a warm personal friend and a learned scholar whose place it would be difficult to fill."

APPENDIX.

"It will probably interest others besides Mahommedans to learn that Moulvie Syed Mohammed Ameer Ali Saheb of Durbhungah is about to publish a work on the Moslem Festivals. It will of course embrace the Ramadan and other festivities, giving descriptions and explanations of them which will cause them and their philosophy to be better understood. The book will be dedicated to Sir Steuart Bayley, who has kindly accepted the dedication. The work will be a handy compendium to all who are interested in Islam, and we wish the author every success."—*The Indian Daily News*, Wednesday, October 22, 1890.

Farewell Lyric.—"Besides the book written on the Moslem Festivals, already dedicated to Sir Steuart Bayley and which, as we now understand, is about to be out from the Press of Messrs. H. C. Gangooly & Co., Moulvie Syed Mohammed Ameer Ali of Durbhungah, is composing a Hindustani poem in expression of his sorrow for Sir Steuart's retirement. The poem, when complete, will be presented to His Honor, along with the aforesaid book, which, among other things, will contain portraits of the Queen-Empress, the Viceroy, the Lieutenant-Governor, and of some other notabilities, European or Native. The Moulvie deserves, in every respect, appreciation of the enterprise by his co-religionists in particular and the public in general."—IBID, Thursday, November 27, 1890.

Present of a Portrait.—"His Honour the Lieutenant-Governor of Bengal has favoured Moulvie Syed Mohammed Ameer Ali, of Durbhungah, with a portrait of his, for publishing the same, with the book which the talented young Moulvie has written on Moslem festivals, and which, as previously announced, is shortly to be out from the Press of Messrs. H. C. Gangooly & Co. The portrait which was taken in London, will, when published, present an interesting scene to roaders of the book aforesaid, and we can only congratulate the Moulvie on the compliment so kindly paid to him by the retiring Lieutenant-Governor."—IBID, Thursday, December 4, 1890.

"SIR STEUART BAYLEY.—As previously announced, Moulvie Syed Mohammed Ameer Ali of Durbhungah, who is author of the book entitled 'The Moslem Festivities,' already dedicated to Sir Steuart Bayley, presented at Belvedere on Monday last at 10 A. M. to His Honor the Hindustani poem composed by the Moulvie as an expression of his sorrow for Sir Steuart's departure from India. His Honor, through his Private Secretary, Lieutenant Bayley, has thanked the Moulvie in a letter, dated the 16th instant for this presentation, the first of its kind ever presented to any Lieutenant-Governor before him."— IBID, Saturday, December 20, 1890.

" * THE MOSLEM FESTIVITIES.—In response to a requisition made by the author of this little *brochure* Moulvie Abul Anwar Syed Mohammed Ameer Ali Saheb of Durbhungah, for a photograph of Her Majesty the Queen-Empress to be published along with the book now in the press, Sir Steuart Colvin Bayley has sent from London by the last mail, to the learned Moulvie the following autographic letter, which will be read with interest by Moslems and others :—

Dear Sir,

I have received your letter asking me to obtain for you a photograph of Her Majesty, and permission to publish it. The former can be obtained by application through the regular official channel, that is the Government of Bengal and the Government of India ; which, as you say, would take a long time. It is for you to consider whether it is worth while. I am much obliged for your kind expressions, and am able to say that I have in no way suffered in health since leaving India."

Yours truly,

INDIA OFFICE,   (Sd.)   S. C. BAYLEY.
London, March 8, 1891.

---

* The *Indian Daily News*, Wednesday, April 1, 1891.

" MOSLEM FESTIVITIES.—Under this title, Moulvie Syed Mohammed Ameer Ali of Durbhungah, has in hand a work dealing with the above subject. It will yet be two months before the work is ready for publication. The book is to contain a number of portraits of notable personages connected with India, though their special relation to Mohammedanism is not clear, except perhaps their friendly feeling towards that community—His Excellency the Viceroy, Sir Steuart Bayley, Sir Auckland Colvin, Nawab Sir Abdul Gunny and Nawab Ahsanullah Saheb, and perhaps others. The delay arises from the production of these portraits in England, from which it may be assumed that they will be done in a superior style. It is satisfactory to see a young member of the Mohammedan community devoting himself to the exposition of their customs and the reasons for them, and it is hoped that the result will be encouraging both to himself and others."—IBID, Thursday, February 19, 1891.

" A PARTING GIFT.—Sir Steuart Bayley has asked Moulvie Syed Mohammed Ameer Ali of Durbhungah, to place a photo. of himsel at the beginning of a book entitled the ' Moslem Festivities,' dedicated to His Honour, who has already accepted the dedication. The book will embrace Ramzan, Mohurrum and other festivities."—The *Englishman*, Wednesday, December 8, 1890.

" Sir Steuart Bayley has favoured Moulvie Syed Mohammed Ameer Ali of Durbhungah, with a portrait of His Honour for the purpose of publishing the same with the book, entitled ' The Moslem Festivities,' which the talented young Moulvie has written, and which is about to be issued from the Press of Messrs. H. C. Gangooly & Co., of this city. The book, which has been dedicated to Sir Steuart Bayley, will, when completed, contain accounts of almost all the Mohammedan anniversaries and other celebrations.

Most of the Moulvie's papers on these subjects have already appeared in the columns of the *Indian Daily News* and the *Statesman*. The book will serve as a handy compendium to those having an interest in Islamitic matters."—The *Indian Mirror*, Wednesday, December 3, 1890.

[75]

"Syed Mohammed Ameer Ali of Bariawl in Durbhungah District, the writer of the interesting series of articles, which appeared lately in the columns of a contemporary headed 'Moslem Festivities,' and a reprint of which is about to be published by Messrs. H. C. Gangooly & Co., had an interview with Sir Charles Elliot, yesterday noon."— The *Indian Mirror*, Sunday, January 10, 1892.

"A Visitor—Among the provincial visitors received by Sir Charles Elliot, on Saturday at Belvedere, was Syed Ameer Ali of Bariawl, Durbhungah. This young gentleman is interesting himself in the Press, and especially seeks to expound the principles of Mohammedanism and Islamitic usages. A work written by him on Islamism will shortly be published by Messrs. H. C. Gangooly & Co., of this city, which will give the public an exposition of Islam, and the thoughts of the writer differing from those of the bulk of the bigoted Moslems of the day. We heartily wish the Syed every success in his work."—The *Indian Daily News*, Thursday, January 12, 1892.

A FRIEND'S LETTER.

Gujrat,
Baroda Camp,
27th December 1890.

My Dear Sir,

Not many things in the world could give me greater pleasure than the affectionate tone of your letter which came to hand yesterday. As to the appreciation of your work by me, I must candidly state that it is a compliment which I must repay with interest. The work, which is an elaborate work of great skill, bespeaks of itself. I am the more pleased for its publication as a man of your abilities and parts has deemed it proper to come to the rescue of our holiday— especially the Mohurrum ones, which are given a variety of interpretation by those of other castes and creeds, which is, I believe, the outcome of astounding bigotry and ignorance. I wish you every success in your undertaking. The sooner the book is out, the better it is. I might be, even, content with a copy without any photo. in the since I believe that the image made on the tablet of my heart of the contents of the book would not be easily obliterated, and would serve as a lasting photo of the merits of the Faith and the results of your labour. As to the names of gentlemen who would likely be subscribers to your book—though I cannot positively say they would—I might suggest you some :—

R. M. Syami, Esq., M.A., L.L.B., Solicitor, Bombay.
Budruddin Tayyabji, Esq., Barrister-at-Law, Bombay.
Mohammed Husain Hakim, " " " "
H. H. the Nawab Saheb Bahadur of Radhanpur.
" " " " Palanpur.
" " " " Junagadh.
" " " " Wadasinor.
" " " " Sachin.
H. H. the Maharaja Saheb Bahadur of Baroda.
The Members of the Anjuman-i-Islam of Bombay.
" " " " " Ahmedabad.

I shall, however, try my best to enlarge the sale of your book among the educated Moslems of this part of the country on the receipt of a copy, which I send them over for having a look at it. I hope to get about 50 or 60 copies sold.

(In haste)

Expecting your reply soon,

Yours truly,
(Sd.) NANNUMIA AHMEDMIA,
Assistant Professor of Persian,
Bareda College, Baroda Camp.

To
MOULVIE S. M. AMEER ALI, ESQ.,
(of Durbhungah)
Ripon Lane, Calcutta.